HAWAIIAN
Seashells

ISLAND HERITAGE
Honolulu, Hawai‘i

Contents

5 Acknowledgments
6 Introduction
9 About This Book
11 Diagram of Shell
12 About Collecting

13

CLASS POLYPLACOPHORA
13 CHITONIDAE/
     ISCHNOCHITONIDAE   Coat-of-Mail Shells

16

CLASS GASTROPODA
16	PATELLIDAE	True Limpets
19	FISSURELLIDAE	Keyhole Limpets
22	TROCHIDAE	Top Shells
26	TURBINIDAE/ PHASIANELLIDAE	Turban Shells and Pheasant Shells
30	NERITIDAE	Nerites
33	LITTORINIDAE	Periwinkles
36	CERITHIIDAE	Horn Shells
41	STROMBIDAE	True Conchs
45	XENOPHORIDAE	Carrier Shells
48	TRIVIIDAE	Trivias
52	CYPRAEIDAE	Cowries

66	OVULIDAE	Ovulids
69	NATICIDAE	Moon Shells
73	CASSIDAE	Helmet Shells
77	TONNIDAE	Tun Shells
81	RANELLIDAE/PERSONIDAE	Tritons
88	BURSIDAE	Frog Shells
92	EULIMIDAE	Obelisk Shells
96	TRIPHORIDAE	Triphorids
101	EPITONIIDAE	Wentletraps
104	JANTHINIDAE	Purple Sea Snails
107	MURICIDAE	Murex Shells
112	THAIDIDAE	Rock Shells
118	CORALLIOPHILIDAE	Coral Shells
123	BUCCINIDAE	Whelks
127	NASSARIIDAE	Basket Shells
131	FASCIOLARIIDAE	Spindle Shells
137	COLUMBELLIDAE	Dove Shells
141	COLUBRARIIDAE	False Tritons
144	OLIVIDAE	Olive Shells
147	HARPIDAE	Harp Shells
150	MITRIDAE	Miters
160	COSTELLARIIDAE	Ribbed Miters
167	TURRIDAE/CLAVINIDAE	Turrids
173	CONIDAE	Cone Shells
187	TEREBRIDAE	Augers
200	ARCHITECTONICIDAE	Sundials
204	PYRAMIDELLIDAE	Pyramid Shells
207	ACTAEONIDAE/BULLINIDAE	Pupa Shells and Bullinids
210	HYDATINIDAE/ CYLICHNIDAE/ HAMINOEIDAE/BULLIDAE	Paper Bubbles, Cylindrical Bubbles, White Bubbles and True Bubbles

CLASS BIVALVIA

214

214	ARCIDAE	Ark Clams
217	GLYCYMERIDIDAE	Bittersweet Clams
221	MYTILIDAE	Marine Mussels
224	PINNIDAE	Pen Shells
227	PTERIIDAE	Pearl Oysters
230	PECTINIDAE	Scallops
234	SPONDYLIDAE	Thorny Oysters
237	LIMIDAE	File Clams
240	CHAMIDAE	Jewel Boxes
243	LUCINIDAE	Saucer Clams
246	CARDIIDAE	Cockles
249	TELLINIDAE	Tellin Clams
252	PSAMMOBIIDAE	Sunset Clams
255	GLOSSIDAE	Oxheart Clams
257	VENERIDAE	Venus Clams

CLASS SCAPHOPODA

260

260	DENTALIIDAE	Tusk Shells

263 Glossary
264 About the Author
265 Common Names Index
270 Scientific Names Index
277 References

Acknowledgments

I would foremost like to thank my wife Pauline Fiene-Severns for her keen editorial advice, assistance, comments and support throughout the preparation of the book. Thanks also to Cory Pittman for the loan of some of the micro species and their identifications. I would also like to thank Dr. E. A. Kay for confirming the confusion over the identity of the Maui Spindle which remains in its own "black hole."

I would especially like to thank Richard Goldberg who enthusiastically and unselfishly helped me with photographic techniques needed to produce this book. Rich also undertook the task of photographing the cowrie section - which he said he enjoyed!

Introduction

The Hawaiian Islands lie near the center of the vast Pacific Ocean just south of the Tropic of Cancer over a thousand miles from their nearest island neighbor, tiny Palmyra Atoll to the south. Yet, in spite of Hawaii's isolation and barely tropical climate it hosts a remarkable number of tropical marine shell species, many of which have adapted to the Hawaiian conditions and become distinct species. These are Hawaii's endemic shell species and they are a testament to Hawaii's long isolation. Among them are the rare and elegant Hawaiian stromb and as many as seven species of cowries found no other place in the world. These endemics and other oddly Hawaiian forms of more widespread species constitute almost one-fifth of the marine shells known from the Hawaiian Islands and distinguish any assemblage of Hawaiian marine shells.

An interesting aspect of Hawaii's marine shells is that some species routinely differ from populations of the same species in other parts of the Pacific and can readily be identified as being from Hawaii. Hawaiian specimens may reach an unusually large size, develop richer colors or possess more marked sculpturing in the shell. These "Hawaiian" characteristics are all just part of the process that can lead to the evolution of another Hawaiian endemic.

Hawaiian mollusks, both terrestrial and aquatic, have been keenly cataloged for the last two centuries by collectors, museum staff, university students and school children, and yet new species are turning up all the time. The number of known octopus species in Hawaii, for example, has almost quadrupled in the last few years to an amazing nineteen species. Another group growing astoundingly in numbers of known species is the micro-mollusks. A virtual deluge of new species found by microscope-bound biologists and graduate students looking through sand samples has been described in recent years. Now it seems many shell enthusiasts no longer walk the beach at low tide, snorkel or dive to make their discoveries. Instead, many serious students of marine shells have turned to collecting sand samples to search for the dead shells of new and often spectacular species.

Other research is changing the names of many species as old, often obscure literature, is reviewed and invalid descriptions come to light. Names are now being questioned as molluscan families are systematically reviewed, and species are re-assigned to new genera or even families with the aid of careful study and the help of DNA analysis. It is not unusual for a species to have been named, not once, but several times, especially if it is a highly variable species (a problem DNA analysis can sort out very quickly in some cases). Rapid changes in communication and the way data is stored and accessed is also helping stem the confusion. Hopefully it will not be as common in the future for a species to be described more than once. But with tens of thousands of mollusk species worldwide, some confusion is to be expected.

The Phylum Mollusca is the second-largest group of invertebrates. Only the Phylum Arthropoda, which includes insects, spiders and crustaceans, is larger in number of species. With such large numbers it is not surprising that mollusks are remarkably diverse in shape, size and behavior. In fact some have incredible, if not bizarre, behaviors that are absolutely fascinating. The fantastic, chameleon-like octopus is able to resemble rocks or even other animals, while a 2-inch long, bullet-shaped *Strombus* found in South East Asian waters can "jump" 15 or 20 feet through the water to escape a predator.

Variation in shell shape is also great, as anyone who has picked up shells will have noticed, and this is part of the attraction. The shell is complex and artfully designed but never frivolous. You can ponder every knob, every curve and every spine. Nearly all have a reason for being there. Environmental pressures have shaped all aspects of the shell from its over-all appearance to the smallest details of strength, structure and color. Shells can be streamlined for moving through sand, multi-shelled like the chitons to conform to the topography of their rugged substrate or comprised of a spiraling set of gas-filled chambers like the chambered nautilus, providing weightlessness in the dark ocean depths. The designs of these shells are the means to their survival with the added benefit of a mysterious, often elegant beauty.

Marine mollusks are sought for food by many animals including man, who considers some to be delicacies rather than just plain "food." Tasty littoral mollusks such as clams and scallops are probably what brought shells into early human camps later to be fashioned into tools. Drills were made from the aptly-named auger shells, while lures, hooks and adzes were made from various clams. Horns were made from the helmet shell and the Triton's trumpet to call the people together or to scatter them to hide from an enemy. Shells such as the nautilus were handy, and are still used to bail canoes and ladle fresh water in Indonesia where the dead shells commonly drift onto beaches.

Shells have even played an important role in human dispersal. It is believed that humans learned to swim and travel across water initially in search of littoral food sources, such as the abundant mollusks found on reef flats at low tide. As nearshore stocks were depleted by wading foragers, offshore stocks beckoned, as did the bountiful reefs of nearby islands. It is easy to imagine the progression of nomadic people from land-locked to island-hopping following the food supplied by low tide. Large mounds of midden consisting primarily of mollusk shells can be found along the coast almost anywhere hunter-gatherer peoples lived and had access to the sea.

Not all mollusks are benign creatures ripe for the picking by low tide hunters though. Some cone shells defend themselves against attack by firing a venomous barb normally used to capture fish or kill other mollusks. The venom squeezed from a gland behind the barb of a fish-eating cone must quickly subdue its prey before it can escape and thus must be very toxic. One, *Conus geographus* can, and has, killed people, while other cone species have sent people reeling in pain because they felt some urge to pick one up for one reason or another. That a marine shell feeds on fish is as remarkable to me as it would be for a garden snail to feed on a sparrow. There is a frightening coldness when an invertebrate feeds on a vertebrate. The mental image of sparrow feathers scattered on the ground in my garden makes the concept even more amazing.

seashells are the external skeletons of these diverse mollusks. The snail which made the shell may have been a sedentary grazer, a more active scavenger or a fast-moving predator, but the shell gives none of that away. The shells, always beautiful, are endlessly varied. It is not hard to imagine how mollusks could have evolved so many different specializations, both in shell form and behavior. They have been around for over 500 million years, about 500 times longer than humans and about 50 times longer than the main Hawaiian Islands we see today.

This book was designed as a field guide to the identification of many of the marine shells found in Hawaiian waters. This introduction and the introductions to the families that follow just skim the surface of a vast amount of knowledge that is available on the subject. For a more in-depth look at the marine shells of Hawaii I would suggest picking up a copy of *Hawaiian Marine Shells* by Dr. E. Alison Kay.

About This Book

To study marine mollusks, fish, birds or any other large group of animals, it is often easier to learn the families that exist within that group before tackling the numerous species within each family. Those families within your personal range are naturally the ones you would want to concentrate on first.

Following this reasoning, this book introduces Hawaii's marine shells by emphasizing the families, which have been arranged in phylogenetic order. The species are then listed in alphabetical order (some within subgenera) after their family introduction.

The book is organized so that each family is introduced with a vertical, full-page shot of a detail of a specimen or specimens of that family. This page is followed by an introductory description of the family and a horizontal photograph of a group of species, to give the general gestalt of the family being presented. The individual species of the family that are found in Hawaii follow with brief captions. Each species photograph is a double exposure of the same specimen, and has been lighted to show surface details of the shell.

The book covers 65 families and over 360 species. All of the families are found elsewhere in the Pacific, though all of the species are not. Hawaii's unique situation has resulted in the highest rate of endemic marine mollusk species in the world. At present, an estimated 18% of Hawaii's marine mollusks are found only in Hawaii. This figure will no doubt drop as more is learned about the species found here.

The shells represented in this book cover a huge range of habitats, from parasitic ovulids that live on precious corals 2,000 feet deep, to intertidal species that are abundant in some of the large tide pool systems found scattered throughout the islands. This is done to illustrate the amazing diversity of this group of animals.

CAPTION INFORMATION
COMMON NAME:
Most of the common names were taken from previously published works. In some cases, they were derived from the scientific name. An (E) means that the species is endemic to Hawaii (known only from the Hawaiian Islands).

SCIENTIFIC NAME:
This is the scientific name of the species, beginning with the genus which is capitalized. Sometimes a sub-

genus is given in parentheses, followed by the species name. Occasionally a subspecies name follows the species name. Completing the scientific name is the name of the person(s) who first formally described the species, and the year the description was published. The author's name in parentheses indicates that the originally assigned genus has since been changed.

ADULT SIZE:
The adult size is the height of the specimen photographed or, in cases such as the sundials where the diameter is greater than the height, the size is the diameter of the shell.

DEPTH:
If only one depth is given, it means that little is known about the depth range of the species, and therefore only the depth of the shell pictured is provided. If a depth range is given, it is because the species is known from that range of depths.

NOTES:
Most of the notes include the habitat where the particular specimen photographed was found.

DISTINCTIVE FEATURES

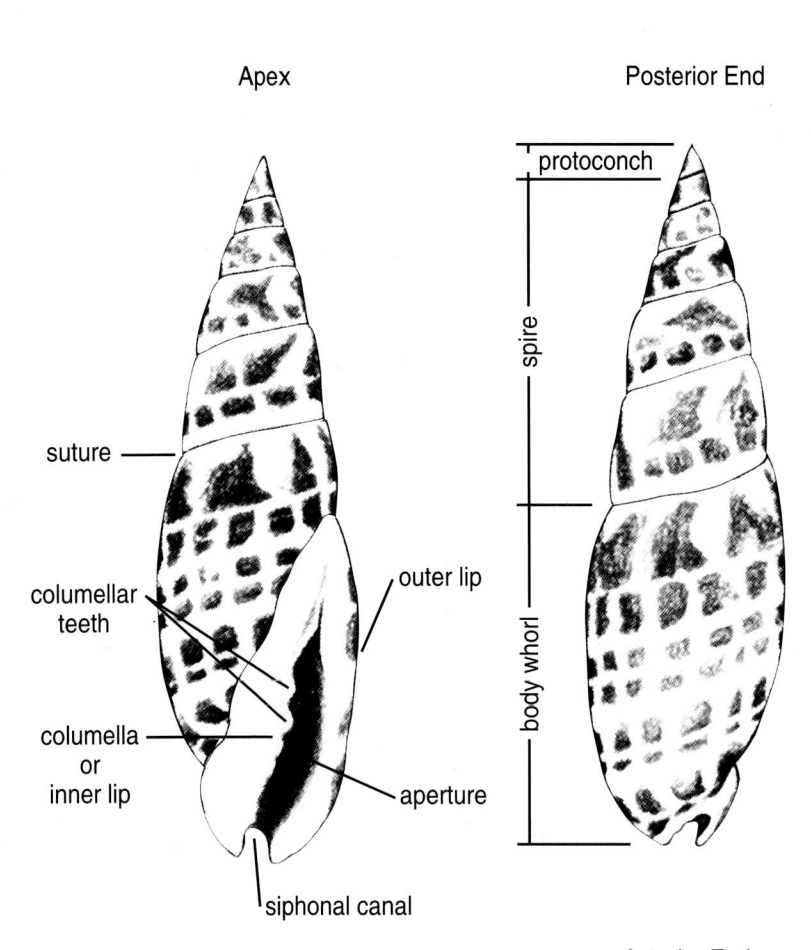

Apex

Posterior End

protoconch

spire

suture

outer lip

columellar teeth

body whorl

columella or inner lip

aperture

siphonal canal

Anterior End

About Collecting:

This book is intended as a guide for divers, snorkelers or beachcombers to help identify shells they may observe as well as shells that they may never have the opportunity to see because the habitat is deep. Many of the shells in this book can be found clean and dead either on the beach or in sandy pockets on the reef where they collect. However, many others are almost always observed alive. Although visually enticing, shells, whether occupied by the original creator or by a hermit crab, are recognized as the homes of living creatures. **Therefore, the collecting of living shells should be avoided.**

CLASS POLYPLACOPHORA

CHITONIDAE/ISCHNOCHITONIDAE —
Coat-of-Mail shells

CLASS POLYPLACOPHORA

CLASS POLYPLACOPHORA

CHITONIDAE/ISCHNOCHITONIDAE — Coat-of-Mail shells

The chitons, or Coat-of Mail shells, are elongate, bilaterally symmetrical mollusks with eight overlapping plates partially embedded in the mantle, which in chitons is called the girdle. The articulating plates allow the chiton to conform to curved surfaces, creating a low profile. A strong, muscular foot provides ordinary adhesion to rocks in areas of heavy surge, but when the chiton is disturbed, the girdle also will clamp down, creating a vacuum and an extraordinary seal. Chitons will remain motionless when exposed at low tide, but will move around to graze on algae and other organisms when submerged by a rising tide. They are especially active at night if the tide is right.

Family: CHITONIDAE
Common Name: Linsley's Chiton
Scientific Name:
Rhyssoplax linsleyi
Burghardt, 1973
Adult Size: 13 mm
Depth: Intertidal to 15 feet
Notes: On smooth rocks

Family: ISCHNOCHITONIDAE
Common Name: Green Chiton
Scientific Name:
Ischnochiton petaloides
(Gould, 1846)
Adult Size: 17 mm
Depth: Intertidal to 10 feet
Notes: Under rubble in windward tide pools

CLASS POLYPLACOPHORA

CLASS GASTROPODA

PATELLIDAE —
True Limpets

CLASS GASTROPODA

PATELLIDAE —
True Limpets

True limpets can be found along exposed rocky shorelines, often above the high tide mark, exposed to air for hours at a time. The conical shell is held against the rock, conserving moisture, but is extended away from the rock when a wave crashes, to allow water to pass over the gills. At high tide, when moisture loss is least likely, they move around grazing on algae. As the tide falls, some species regularly return to a homesite of attachment where they have ground a circular place for themselves in the rock which fits their shell. Years ago, a few mischievous scientists discovered that by changing the shape or surface features of a particular limpet's homesite, they could limit the ability of that limpet to identify it. True limpets, or opihi, are considered the most dangerous form of marine life in Hawaii. Every year, at least one person is swept into the sea by large surf while trying to harvest this delicacy.

Common Name:
Black-mouthed Limpet (E)
Scientific Name:
Cellana melanostoma
(Pilsbry, 1891)
Adult Size: 60 mm
Depth: Intertidal
Notes: In the splash zone, on rocky coasts

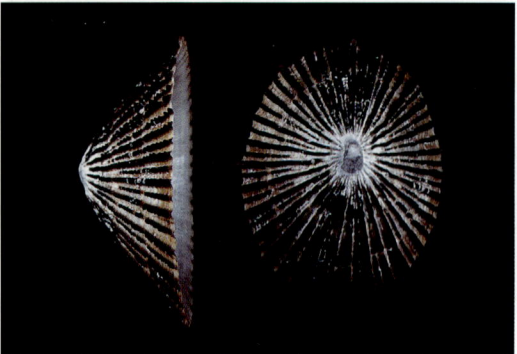

Common Name: Hawaiian Limpet (E)
Scientific Name:
Cellana sandwicensis
(Pease, 1861)
Adult Size: 70 mm
Depth: Intertidal
Notes: In the splash zone, on rocky coasts

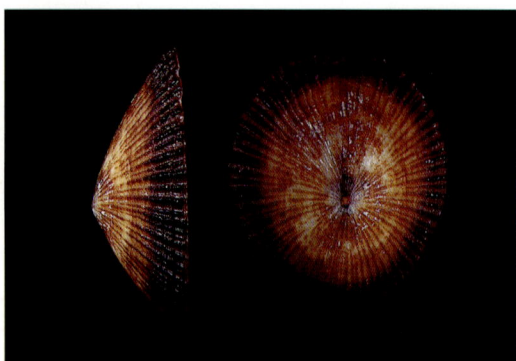

Common Name: Talc Limpet (E)
Scientific Name: *Cellana talcosa*
(Gould, 1846)
Adult Size: 80 mm
Depth: 0 to 30 feet
Notes: On submerged rocks along lava coast

CLASS GASTROPODA

FISSURELLIDAE —
Keyhole Limpets

CLASS GASTROPODA

FISSURELLIDAE —
Keyhole Limpets

Closely related to the true limpets are the keyhole limpets. Their less calcified shells, most of which have a hole at the top or a slit at the front end, are adaptations to life below the low tide mark where moisture loss is not a threat, as it is for the true limpets living higher on the shoreline. Water exits this hole or slit after it has entered under the shell's lip and passed over the gills.

Common Name: Eight-sided Limpet
Scientific Name: *Diodora octagona*
(Reeve, 1850)
Adult Size: 10 mm
Depth: Less than 10 feet
Notes: Attached to the undersides of rocks in shallow water

Common Name: Hawaiian Keyhole Limpet
Scientific Name: *Emarginula dilecta*
A. Adams, 1852
Adult Size: 8 mm
Depth: 10 - 15 feet
Notes: Dead shells can be found in shallow water coral communities

CLASS GASTROPODA

CLASS GASTROPODA

TROCHIDAE —
Top Shells

CLASS GASTROPODA

TROCHIDAE —
Top Shells

Top shells comprise a very large, diverse group of shells found from the shallow water of tide pools down to great depths. They generally have a shell that is thick and strong and, like the limpets, have evolved a high-spired, straight-sided shape that helps them hold on in surgy water. Most graze on seaweed and can be seen crawling about on the reef in shallow water at night. When found by divers, most are heavily encrusted with calcareous deposits, hiding the sculpture and color beneath.

Common Name: Ocellate Top Shell
Scientific Name: *Alcyna ocellata*
Hickman & McLean, 1990
Adult Size: 1.5 mm
Depth: Intertidal to 300 feet
Notes: In tide pools and beyond the reef. Very common in beach sand on protected coasts

Common Name: Doncorn's Top Shell (E)
Scientific Name: *Calliostoma (Tristichotrochus) doncorni*
Kay, 1979
Adult Size: 22 mm
Depth: 1000 feet
Notes: Trawled

Common Name: Top Shell
Scientific Name: *Gaza* sp.
Adult Size: 5 mm
Depth: 1000 feet
Notes: Trawled

Common Name: Marbled Top Shell
Scientific Name:
Gibbula marmorea
(Pease, 1861)
Adult Size: 2 mm
Depth: Intertidal
Notes: Lives on algae-covered rocks in tide pools and on reef flats. Very common in beach sand

Common Name: Top Shell
Scientific Name: *Trochus intextus*
Kiener, 1850
Adult Size: 20 mm
Depth: Intertidal to 40 feet
Notes: Found in rubble

CLASS GASTROPODA

CLASS GASTROPODA

TURBINIDAE/PHASIANELLIDAE —
Turban Shells and Pheasant Shells

CLASS GASTROPODA

CLASS GASTROPODA

TURBINIDAE/PHASIANELLIDAE — Turban Shells and Pheasant Shells

Turban shells are a large family with solid, globose shells that typically live in calm, shallow waters. They can be distinguished from the straight-sided top shells by their inflated appearance. Many seashells have a "trap door" called an operculum, which protects the soft animal when it withdraws into its shell. In the turbans this operculum is heavily calcified (shell-like) and is sometimes called a "cat's eye." The operculum of the top shells is thin and horny. Turban shells feed on microscopic algae by rasping them from hard surfaces, leaving an obvious trail of clean substrate behind them. Accordingly, they are most common on rocky bottoms where algae growth is profuse. Because of their substantial shell, empty turbans are likely to be found unbroken washed up on beaches.

Family: TURBINIDAE
Common Name: Ruby-belted Turban
Scientific Name:
Leptothyra rubricincta
(Mighels, 1845)
Adult Size: 1.5 mm
Depth: Intertidal
Notes: On algae-covered rocks in tide pools and on reef flats. Common in beach sand

Family: TURBINIDAE
Common Name: Wart Turban
Scientific Name:
Leptothyra verruca
(Gould, 1845)
Adult Size: 3 mm
Depth: Intertidal
Notes: On algae-covered rocks in tide pools and on reef flats. Common in beach sand

Family: TURBINIDAE
Common Name: Hawaiian Turban (E)
Scientific Name:
Turbo sandwicensis
Pease, 1861
Adult Size: 90 mm
Depth: 1 - 250 feet
Notes: Under rocks in shallow water

CLASS GASTROPODA

Family: PHASIANELLIDAE
Common Name: Variable Pheasant Shell
Scientific Name:
Tricolia (Hiloa) variabilis
(Pease, 1861)
Adult Size: 1 - 2 mm
Depth: Intertidal to 300 feet
Notes: On algae-covered rocks in tide pools and beyond the reef. Common in beach sand

CLASS GASTROPODA

CLASS GASTROPODA

NERITIDAE —
Nerites

CLASS GASTROPODA

NERITIDAE —
Nerites

Nerites are mainly intertidal species, living along the shoreline attached to rocks, tree roots or man-made structures from the splash zone on down into intertidal waters. Their distinguishing characteristic — a semicircular aperture, straight across one end — can be seen when viewed from beneath. The aperture is also characterized by strong tooth-like structures that are often splashed with color. Nerites are flattened, oval and thick-shelled, which allows them to survive the rugged conditions of the splash zone while remaining near the algae which thrives where sunlight and water exchange are great. Their Hawaiian name, pip-ipi, means small and close together, referring to their dense populations on exposed rocks. Because of this, they have been an abundant, easily-collected food in Hawaii for generations. Some species are eaten after being heated and are plucked from the shell with a sharp stick. Others are eaten raw as an intertidal hors d'oeuvre, but one must first get past a very close-fitting, calcareous operculum which protects the animal when withdrawn.

Common Name: Pipipi Nerite
Scientific Name: *Nerita picea* (Récluz, 1841)
Adult Size: 15 mm
Depth: Supratidal to 3 feet
Notes: Lives on the sides of rocks in tide pools and in the splash zone on rocky shores

Common Name: Pleated Nerite
Scientific Name: *Nerita plicata* Linnaeus, 1758
Adult Size: 18 mm
Depth: Supratidal to 5 feet
Notes: Lives on the sides of rocks in tide pools and in the splash zone on rocky shores. Also on the limbs of trees overhanging water

Common Name: Polished Nerite
Scientific Name: *Nerita polita* Linnaeus, 1758
Adult Size: 30 mm
Depth: Intertidal to 6 feet
Notes: Lives under sand during the day, but emerges at night to graze

CLASS GASTROPODA

LITTORINIDAE —
Periwinkles

CLASS GASTROPODA

LITTORINIDAE —
Periwinkles

Periwinkles are the shells most likely to be seen on rocks of the high shoreline where they graze on fine algae. Although capable of living above the high tide mark for long periods of time, they are tied to the ocean by the need to keep their gills moist and by their mode of reproduction. After mating, females shed fertilized eggs into the ocean where development takes place. Because they live exposed, they are rather small and drab so as not to attract the attention of predators, such as birds. Some species can be found living on the limbs of trees surprisingly high out of the water. The name "periwinkle" comes from the Elizabethan words "penny winkle," meaning small whelks that cost a penny per handful. Hawaiians harvested these shells for food, as they were concentrated in large numbers and easily plucked from rocks.

Common Name: Speckled Periwinkle
Scientific Name: *Littoraria pintado* (Wood, 1828)
Adult Size: 20 mm
Depth: Supratidal
Notes: Above the water line on rocks and breakwalls, and on the sides of rocks in tide pools

---

Common Name: Rough Periwinkle
Scientific Name: *Littoraria scabra* (Linnaeus, 1758)
Adult Size: 30 mm
Depth: Supratidal
Notes: Above the water line on rocks and on the roots and limbs of trees overhanging the water

Common Name: Pease's Periwinkle
Scientific Name: *Peasiella tantilla* (Gould, 1849)
Adult Size: 5 mm
Depth: Supratidal to 5 feet
Notes: Above the water line on rocks and on the sides of rocks in tide pools

CLASS GASTROPODA

CLASS GASTROPODA

CERITHIIDAE —
Horn Shells

CLASS GASTROPODA

CERITHIIDAE —
Horn Shells

Horn shells are a large group characterized by an up-turned siphonal canal that protects the siphon and allows them to live just beneath the surface of the sand. They are some of the most commonly-seen seashells in shallow water, living in large colonies. At shallow depths the smaller species prefer to live in sand pockets and calm, protected bays while the larger species are normally found in open sand beyond the reef. The shallow-water dwellers can best be seen in the early morning before wind-driven waves and tides obliterate the trails left in the sand from the evening's foraging. The trails of deeper-water dwellers can be found throughout the day. All are algae and detritus feeders and are common prey for predatory mollusks, especially moon shells, which drill a hole through the shell and extract the animal. Hundreds of drilled horn shells can sometimes be seen on the reef flat at low tide occupied by hermit crabs.

Common Name: Overhanging Horn
Scientific Name:
Bittium impendens
(Hedley, 1899)
Adult Size: 10 mm
Depth: Intertidal to 60 feet
Notes: Most common in tide pools. Dead shells are abundant in sand shoreward of fringing reefs

Common Name: Column Horn
Scientific Name:
Cerithium columna
Sowerby, 1834
Adult Size: 35 mm
Depth: Intertidal to 300 feet
Notes: A common species in sand pockets and tide pools

Common Name: Prickly Horn
Scientific Name:
Cerithium echinatum
Houbrick, 1992
Adult Size: 47 mm
Depth: Intertidal to 300 feet
Notes: Most common in shallow water where it lives in sand and rubble areas

CLASS GASTROPODA

Common Name: Beaked Horn
Scientific Name:
Cerithium rostratum
Sowerby, 1855
Adult Size: 22 mm
Depth: 10 - 100 feet
Notes: Lives in sand pockets

Common Name: Articulate Horn
Scientific Name:
Rhinoclavis articulata
(Adams & Reeve, 1850)
Adult Size: 35 mm
Depth: 3 - 480 feet
Notes: Lives in open sand

Common Name: Banded Horn
Scientific Name:
Rhinoclavis fasciata
(Bruguière, 1792)
Adult Size: 70 mm
Depth: 45 - 600 feet
Notes: Lives in open sand

Common Name: Chinese Horn
Scientific Name:
Rhinoclavis sinensis
(Gmelin, 1791)
Adult Size: 58 mm
Depth: Intertidal to 45 feet
Notes: Lives in open sand

CLASS GASTROPODA

STROMBIDAE —
True Conchs

CLASS GASTROPODA

STROMBIDAE —
True Conchs

Stromboids get their name from the U-shaped (stromboid) notch at the anterior end of the outer lip. One of the eyes is held upright, protruding through the notch in the shell while the other is kept low, beneath the lip of the shell. Well-developed, the eyes respond quickly to movement and light changes, which might signal danger. True conchs are herbivorous and usually shallow-water dwellers. Many species are edible and they were a common food source for Hawaiians. The true conchs have several unusual means of locomotion. One species, *Strombus maculatus,* has been recorded to leap farther than one meter by digging its large operculum into the bottom and catapulting itself off the bottom.

Common Name: Three-toothed Stromb
Scientific Name:
Strombus dentatus
Linnaeus, 1758
Adult Size: 42 mm
Depth: 45 - 240 feet
Notes: Lives in sand near or among rocks and coral rubble

Common Name: Hell's Stromb (E)
Scientific Name: *Strombus helli*
Kiener, 1843
Adult Size: 23 mm
Depth: 40 - 300 feet
Notes: Lives in sand near or among pen shells

Common Name: Spotted Stromb
Scientific Name:
Strombus maculatus
Sowerby, 1842
Adult Size: 32 mm
Depth: Intertidal to 10 feet
Notes: Lives in sand near coral rubble and under rocks on sand bottom

CLASS GASTROPODA

Common Name: Hawaiian Stromb (E)
Scientific Name:
Strombus vomer hawaiensis
Pilsbry, 1917
Adult Size: 120 mm
Depth: 75 - 1000 feet
Notes: Lives buried in sand

CLASS GASTROPODA

XENOPHORIDAE —
Carrier Shells

CLASS GASTROPODA

XENOPHORIDAE —
Carrier Shells

Carrier shells are a very old group which has been around since the Cretaceous period 135 million years ago. They have the amazing habit of cementing empty shells, coral or stones to their own shells with a type of nacreous glue secreted by the mantle as the shell forms. This bizarre practice may have begun as a protective measure, camouflaging the carrier shell from predators. A species not found in Hawaii attaches branching sponges a half a meter high! Several adaptations indicate a life on silty bottom, among them a muscular foot which moves them around on the bottom in a jerky, leaping motion, and powerful currents produced in the mantle cavity for keeping the cavity free of silt. Their silt habitat is further confirmed by the shell species they have attached to their shells which also inhabit silty bottom. They are mostly brought to light in trawls from very deep water and therefore information on their habits and behavior is limited.

Common Name: Peron's Carrier Shell
Scientific Name:
Xenophora peroniana
(Iredale, 1929)
Adult Size: 50 mm
Depth: 60 - 1300 feet
Notes: Trawled on sand

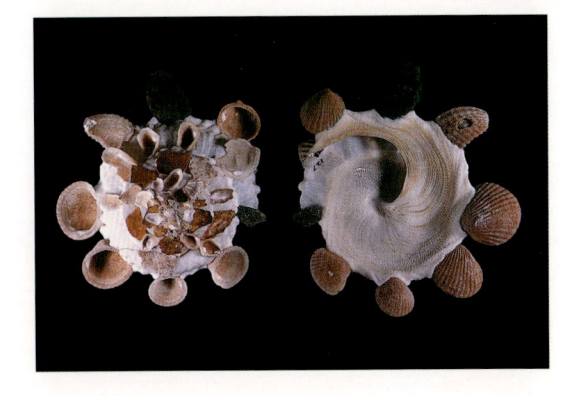

CLASS GASTROPODA

CLASS GASTROPODA

TRIVIIDAE —
Trivias

CLASS GASTROPODA

TRIVIIDAE —
Trivias

Trivias are often associated with cowries (Cypraeidae) because of their ovate shells, but their shells differ from those of cowries by being sculptured with intricate corrugations. The distinct nature of the corrugated patterns of each trivia species can be used as a key to identify the Hawaiian species. Trivias prey on colonial ascidians which can be found on the undersides of rocks and in cracks in the reef. They feed by inserting their long proboscis into one of the zooids and drawing out nutrients. Most of Hawaii's trivia species are common in beach drift, indicating a shallow habitat, though one species is known to live as deep as 100 feet. Trivia species found in Hawaii are very small, not exceeding 5 mm.

Common Name: Edgar's Trivia
Scientific Name: *Trivia edgari* Shaw, 1909
Adult Size: 4 mm
Depth: 30 - 100 feet
Notes: Found in cracks and under rocks

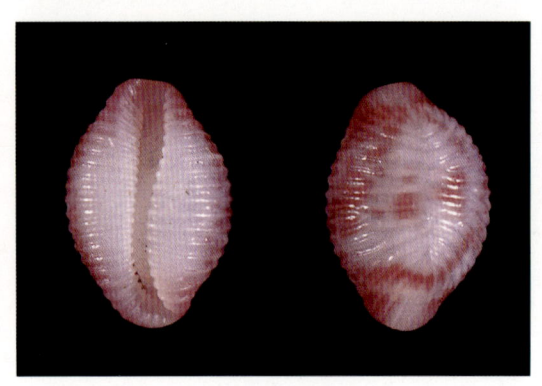

Common Name: Small Trivia
Scientific Name: *Trivia exigua* Gray, 1831
Adult Size: 5 mm
Depth: 10 - 50 feet
Notes: Found in cracks and under rocks

Common Name: White-ribbed Trivia
Scientific Name: *Trivia hordacea* Kiener, 1845
Adult Size: 5 mm
Depth: Intertidal
Notes: Found under rocks. Common locally in beach sand

CLASS GASTROPODA

Common Name: Transparent Trivia
Scientific Name: *Trivia pellucidula* Reeve, 1846
Adult Size: 5 mm
Depth: 60 feet
Notes: Found in cracks and under rocks

CLASS GASTROPODA

CYPRAEIDAE —
Cowries

CLASS GASTROPODA

CYPRAEIDAE —
Cowries

Cowries have long been prized by collectors for their highly polished shells, beautiful colors and intricate patterns. The common name cowrie began as "kauri," the Hindu word for shells where in India they were used as currency as early as 900 A.D. Their use has been documented even earlier in China – in the 14th century B.C. Cypraea moneta, the "money cowrie," was used primarily but other small, easily-gathered cowries were used as well.

Cowries are characterized by their globose and glossy shells, narrow aperture and toothed lips. They live from the intertidal to over 100 meters. Some large cowries may live 10 years or more and small ones two or three years. They may remain in a small area during their relatively long life with most species active at night. After mating, the female lays her eggs in a protected depression or under a rock, and broods them by sitting for days with her foot spread over them. At first the eggs are white, but as they mature they will darken.

The beautiful luster of cowrie shells owes itself to the two lobes of the mantle which extend up on either side covering and protecting the shell. When moving about, the mantle helps to camouflage the shell with its many projecting papillae. These papillae also function in respiration by adding surface area to the mantle, increasing oxygen exchange. Most cowries feed on algae, sponges or dead animals such as fish, urchins or shrimp. The narrow, toothy slit on the underside makes it difficult for predators to get at the animal, but they still fall prey to the occasional octopus which relishes the larger cowries. In Hawaii, cowrie shells are still used as part of a lure to catch octopus.

Common Name: Marie's Cowrie
Scientific Name:
Cypraea (Annepona) mariae
Schilder, 1927
Adult Size: 20 mm
Depth: 15 feet
Notes: Found deep in cracks at night

Common Name: Rashleigh's Cowrie
Scientific Name:
Cypraea (Blasicrura) rashleighana rashleighana
 Melvill, 1888
Adult Size: 20 mm
Depth: 40 - 160 feet
Notes: Beneath rocks

Common Name: Tapering Cowrie
Scientific Name:
Cypraea (Blasicrura) teres pellucens
Melvill, 1888
Adult Size: 30 mm
Depth: 10 - 60 feet
Notes: Beneath rocks

CLASS GASTROPODA

Common Name: Gaskoin's Cowrie (E)
Scientific Name:
Cypraea (Cribrarula) gaskoini
Reeve, 1846
Adult Size: 30 mm
Depth: 20 - 200 feet
Notes: Beneath rocks

Common Name: Tiger Cowrie
Scientific Name:
Cypraea (Cypraea) tigris
Linnaeus, 1758
Adult Size: 130 mm
Depth: Intertidal to 150 feet
Notes: In cracks or out among rocks

Common Name: Beck's Cowrie
Scientific Name:
Cypraea (Erosaria) beckii
Gaskoin, 1836
Adult Size: 14 mm
Depth: 160 - 240 feet
Notes: In the bases of black coral trees

Common Name: Snake's Head Cowrie
Scientific Name:
Cypraea (Erosaria) caputserpentis caputophidii
Schilder, 1927
Adult Size: 35 mm
Depth: Intertidal
Notes: In cracks on wave benches and under rocks

Common Name: Waxy Cowrie
Scientific Name:
Cypraea (Erosaria) cernica
Sowerby, 1870
Adult Size: 34 mm
Depth: 80 - 300 feet
Notes: Beneath rocks

Common Name: Eroded Cowrie
Scientific Name:
Cypraea (Erosaria) erosa
Linnaeus, 1758
Adult Size: 38 mm
Depth: 2 feet
Notes: Beneath a rock

CLASS GASTROPODA

Common Name: Granulated Cowrie (E)
Scientific Name:
Cypraea (Erosaria) granulata
Pease, 1862
Adult Size: 38 mm
Depth: 5 - 100 feet
Notes: Beneath rocks, in caves and deep in cracks

Common Name: Honey Cowrie
Scientific Name:
Cypraea (Erosaria) helvola hawaiiensis
Melvill, 1888
Adult Size: 25 mm
Depth: 5 - 100 feet
Notes: Beneath rocks

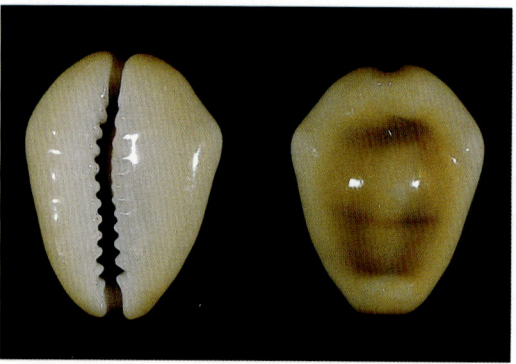

Common Name: Money Cowrie
Scientific Name:
Cypraea (Erosaria) moneta
Linnaeus, 1758
Adult Size: 32 mm
Depth: Intertidal
Notes: In cracks and beneath rocks in tidepools and on reef flats

Common Name: Nuclear Cowrie
Scientific Name:
Cypraea (Erosaria) nucleus
Linnaeus, 1758
Adult Size: 24 mm
Depth: 2 - 80 feet
Notes: In silt at base of finger coral (*Porites compressa*)

Common Name: Ostergaard's Cowrie (E)
Scientific Name:
Cypraea (Erosaria) ostergaardi
Dall, 1921
Adult Size: 24 mm
Depth: 80 - 130 feet
Notes: Beneath rocks

Common Name: Porous Cowrie
Scientific Name:
Cypraea (Erosaria) poraria
Linnaeus, 1758
Adult Size: 24 mm
Depth: 10 - 20 feet
Notes: Associated with dead coral

CLASS GASTROPODA

Common Name: Half-Swimmer Cowrie (E)
Scientific Name:
Cypraea (Erosaria) semiplota
Mighels, 1845
Adult Size: 20 mm
Depth: 10 - 75 feet
Notes: Under coral and rocks

Common Name: Chinese Cowrie
Scientific Name:
Cypraea (Erronea) chinensis amiges
Melvill & Standen, 1904
Adult Size: 40 mm
Depth: 15 - 75 feet.
Notes: Under rocks

Common Name: Children's Cowrie
Scientific Name:
Cypraea (Ipsa) childreni
Gray, 1825
Adult Size: 20 mm
Depth: Unknown
Notes: Known in Hawaii only from subfossils

Common Name: Isabelle's Cowrie
Scientific Name:
Cypraea (Luria) isabella controversa
Gray, 1824
Adult Size: 42 mm
Depth: Intertidal to 250 feet
Notes: Beneath rocks

Common Name: Checkered Cowrie (E)
Scientific Name:
Cypraea (Luria) tessellata
Swainson, 1822
Adult Size: 42 mm
Depth: 20 - 120 feet
Notes: Beneath rocks

Common Name: Carnelian Cowrie
Scientific Name:
Cypraea (Lyncina) carneola propinqua
Garrett, 1879
Adult Size: 56 mm
Depth: 10 - 60 feet
Notes: Beneath rocks

CLASS GASTROPODA

Common Name: Leviathan Cowrie
Scientific Name:
Cypraea (Lyncina) leviathan
Schilder & Schilder, 1937
Adult Size: 83 mm
Depth: Intertidal to 25 feet
Notes: Under rocks or in shaded areas such as caves and arches

Common Name: Lynx Cowrie
Scientific Name:
Cypraea (Lyncina) lynx
Linnaeus, 1758
Adult Size: 50 mm
Depth: 2 - 10 feet
Notes: Beneath rocks

Common Name: Schilders' Cowrie
Scientific Name:
Cypraea (Lyncina) schilderorum
(Iredale, 1939)
Adult Size: 35 mm
Depth: 10 - 70 feet.
Notes: Beneath rocks

Common Name: Grooved Tooth Cowrie (E)
Scientific Name:
Cypraea (Lyncina) sulcidentata
Gray, 1824
Adult Size: 50 mm
Depth: 5 - 120 feet
Notes: Beneath rocks

Common Name: Calf Cowrie
Scientific Name:
Cypraea (Lyncina) vitellus
Linnaeus, 1758
Adult Size: 68 mm
Depth: 2 - 10 feet
Notes: Beneath rocks

Common Name: Reticulated Cowrie
Scientific Name:
Cypraea (Mauritia) maculifera
Schilder, 1932
Adult Size: 78 mm
Depth: 2 - 50 feet
Notes: In cracks and shaded areas

CLASS GASTROPODA

Common Name: Humpback Cowrie
Scientific Name:
Cypraea (Mauritia) mauritiana
Linnaeus, 1758
Adult Size: 114 mm
Depth: 2 - 30 feet
Notes: In cracks and on rocks in high-surge areas

Common Name: Jester Cowrie
Scientific Name:
Cypraea (Mauritia) scurra indica
Gmelin, 1791
Adult Size: 50 mm
Depth: 10 - 40 feet
Notes: Out at night on coral

Common Name: Chick-Pea Cowrie
Scientific Name:
Cypraea (Pustularia) cicercula
Linnaeus, 1758
Adult Size: 20 mm
Depth: Intertidal to 30 feet
Notes: Out at night

Common Name: Maui's Cowrie (E)
Scientific Name:
Cypraea (Pustularia) mauiensis
Burgess, 1967
Adult Size: 15 mm
Depth: Intertidal to 10 feet
Notes: Out at night

Common Name: Fringed Cowrie
Scientific Name:
Cypraea (Purpuradusta) fimbriata
Gmelin, 1791
Adult Size: 14 mm
Depth: 10 - 60 feet
Notes: Beneath rocks

Common Name: Mole Cowrie
Scientific Name:
Cypraea (Talparia) talpa
Linnaeus, 1758
Adult Size: 87 mm
Depth: 10 - 250 feet.
Notes: Beneath rocks and in deep cracks

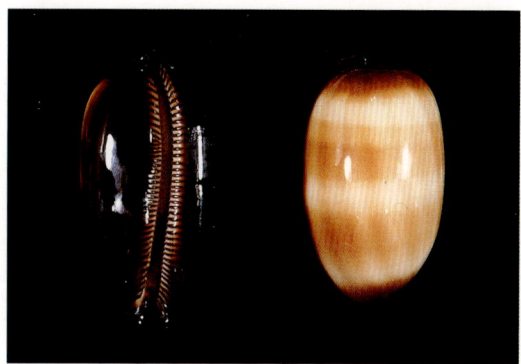

CLASS GASTROPODA

CLASS GASTROPODA

OVULIDAE —
Ovulids

CLASS GASTROPODA

OVULIDAE —
Ovulids

Also known as allied cowries, the ovulids differ from cowries by their more extended ends, lack of a toothed aperture and lack of detailed color patterns. The shells of most ovulids are somewhat glossy because, like the cowries, the mantle covers the shell and keeps encrusting organisms from living on it. Unlike many cowries, however, the mantle covers the shell even when the ovulid is inactive. They are all carnivorous, the six Hawaiian species feeding on wire coral, other species of black corals, and precious corals (gorgonaceans). Ovulids lay their eggs on their host, either on the trunk of the coral or on the limbs of some branching black corals. This is often the only way their presence is detected. All six species in Hawaii inhabit deep water.

Common Name: Schilders' Ovulid
Scientific Name:
Margovula sp. cf. *schilderorum*
C. N. Cate, 1973
Adult Size: 18 mm
Depth: 2000 feet
Notes: Associated with precious corals

Common Name: Weaver's Ovulid
Scientific Name:
Phenacovolva weaveri
C. N. Cate, 1973
Adult Size: 17 mm
Depth: 170 feet
Notes: Associated with black corals

CLASS GASTROPODA

NATICIDAE —
Moon Shells

CLASS GASTROPODA

NATICIDAE —
Moon Shells

Rarely seen, moon shells are sand-dwellers which lay a distinctively-shaped egg mass at night consisting of eggs, sand and mucus molded together into a flat, flexible collar. The moon shell then retreats into the sand, leaving the eggs exposed. The animal is usually uniformly white, large and slimy and is often too big to fit entirely inside the shell. It lives in darkness beneath the sand, pulling itself along with a broad foot. Sand is kept out of the mantle cavity by the foot which covers the head region. Because the shell is always under sand or encased by the animal, the shells are kept glossy and free from encrustation. They prey on other seashells, including horn shells, by boring a hole through the shell using a chemical secreted at the tip of the proboscis. This hole is the trademark of moon shell predation and if a dead shell is found with a conical hole in its side, then you can suspect its demise was precipitated by a moon shell.

Common Name: Butterfly Moon Shell
Scientific Name: *Natica alapapilionis* (Roding, 1798)
Adult Size: 26 mm
Depth: 500 - 1000 feet
Notes: Trawled

Common Name: Arrow Moon Shell
Scientific Name: *Natica gualteriana* Récluz, 1844
Adult Size: 15 mm
Depth: 0 - 300 feet
Notes: In sand in tide pools and beyond the reef

Common Name: Cheerful Moon Shell
Scientific Name: *Natica hilaris* Sowerby, 1914
Adult Size: 28 mm
Depth: 240 - 1000 feet
Notes: Trawled

CLASS GASTROPODA

Common Name: Opaque Moon Shell
Scientific Name: *Polinices melanostomus* (Gmelin, 1791)
Adult Size: 16 mm
Depth: 30 - 110 feet
Notes: In sand

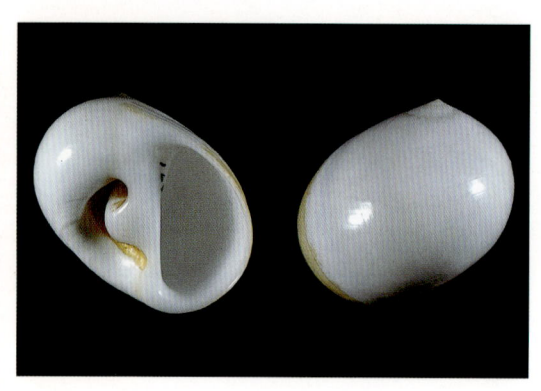

Common Name: Elephant's Foot Moon Shell
Scientific Name: *Polinices peselephanti* (Link, 1807)
Adult Size: 40 mm
Depth: 120 - 500 feet
Notes: In sand

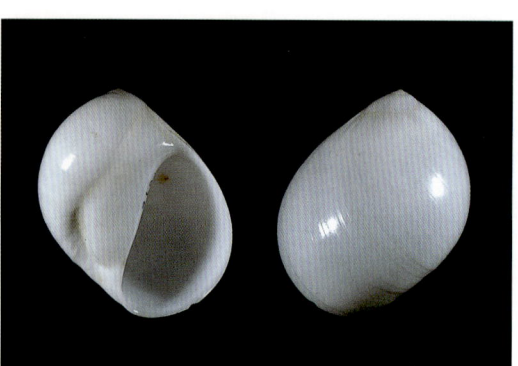

Common Name: Pear-shaped Moon Shell
Scientific Name: *Polinices tumidus* (Swainson, 1840)
Adult Size: 40 mm
Depth: 30 - 250 feet
Notes: In sand

CLASS GASTROPODA

CASSIDAE —
Helmet Shells

CLASS GASTROPODA

CASSIDAE —
Helmet Shells

Most members of this family are small sand-dwellers, but there are a few members that grow to impressive sizes and weights. The shells are heavily calcified and have teeth either just inside the lip or along the very outer edge. In the case of the horned helmet, *Cassis cornuta,* the males can be distinguished from the females by the height of the horns. Long-horned shells are males and short-horned shells are females. This is one of the few seashells large enough to have been used by Hawaiians as a trumpet. Helmets live mostly on open sand bottoms where they sometimes spend time buried in the sand. Their prey consists primarily of sand-dwelling sea urchins and sand dollars which they locate chemically. After the prey is located, they begin by removing the spines from an area on the urchin or sand dollar, then bore a hole through which to extract the animal. A wake of empty urchin tests can often lead right to the responsible helmet shell.

Common Name: Vibex Helmet
Scientific Name:
Casmaria erinaceus kalosmodix
(Melvill, 1883)
Adult Size: 55 mm
Depth: 60 - 120 feet
Notes: Deep in sand

Common Name: Ponderous Helmet
Scientific Name:
Casmaria ponderosa
(Gmelin, 1791)
Adult Size: 45 mm
Depth: 80 - 100 feet
Notes: In sand

Common Name: Horned Helmet
Scientific Name: *Cassis cornuta*
(Linnaeus, 1758)
Adult Size: 285 mm (11 inches)
Depth: 10 - 200 feet
Notes: On or in sand

CLASS GASTROPODA

Common Name: Bubble Helmet
Scientific Name:
Phalium (Semicassis) bulla
(Habe, 1961)
Adult Size: 78 mm
Depth: 200 - 1000 feet
Notes: Trawled on sand

Common Name: Grooved Helmet (E)
Scientific Name:
Phalium (Semicassis) umbilicatum
(Pease, 1861)
Adult Size: 75 mm
Depth: 60 - 1000 feet
Notes: Trawled on sand

CLASS GASTROPODA

TONNIDAE —
Tun Shells

CLASS GASTROPODA

TONNIDAE —
Tun Shells

Tun shells are characterized by their clean, thin, globular shells which usually have complex color patterns. In the case of *Tonna perdix,* this has led to the choice of its scientific name. Perdix means quail-like and refers to the distinctive pattern on the shell. Most tun shells are large, and it is hard to believe that shells of this size live under the sand, but they do! They move about much the same as the moon shells described earlier, and like the moon shells, the tun shell animals are so large that many cannot fit into their own shell.

They are subtle hunters, coming out of the sand at night to feed on sleeping fish, echinoderms and crustaceans by creeping up and pouncing on them with their large foot. They have been seen traveling across the bottom at more than a snail's pace and can move very quickly to bury themselves in the sand when threatened. There is rarely a trace left on the surface of the sand after burying themselves, and therefore the only time one is likely to encounter a living tun shell is at night.

Common Name: Apple Tun
Scientific Name: *Malea pomum*
(Linnaeus, 1758)
Adult Size: 75 mm
Depth: 50 to 1000 feet
Notes: In sand

Common Name: Barrel Tun
Scientific Name: *Tonna dolium*
(Linnaeus, 1758)
Adult Size: 110 mm
Depth: 100 - 200 feet
Notes: In sand

Common Name: Black-mouthed Tun
Scientific Name:
Tonna melanostoma
(Jay, 1839)
Adult Size: 190 mm
Depth: 160 - 300 feet
Notes: In sand

CLASS GASTROPODA

Common Name: Partridge Tun
Scientific Name: *Tonna perdix* (Linnaeus, 1758)
Adult Size: 140 mm
Depth: 10 - 180 feet
Notes: In sand near rocks or out on rocks at night

CLASS GASTROPODA

RANELLIDAE/PERSONIDAE —
Tritons

CLASS GASTROPODA

CLASS GASTROPODA

RANELLIDAE/PERSONIDAE —
Tritons

Some of the world's largest living seashells are included in this family which contains the triton's trumpet, Charonia tritonis, the largest seashell in Hawaii, sometimes reaching 50 cm! Although there are many species of triton, the triton's trumpet is by far the most well-known. It is the shell most often used as a horn by Hawaiians because of its size, beauty and the clear notes that can be produced. Triton's trumpets are predators, feeding on a variety of mollusks, starfish and worms. Watching a triton's trumpet sense and track its prey is an education. It seems to come alive when it picks up the chemical signature of its prey, first extending from its shell, then following the chemical scent quickly until it reaches the prey and grabs it with its powerful foot. Then, like all tritons, it secretes a powerful, paralyzing acid from glands in its proboscis and slowly begins to digest its unlucky prey. Triton's trumpets are long-lived and can be seen in one area for long periods of time.

Family: RANELLIDAE
Common Name: Triton's Trumpet
Scientific Name: *Charonia tritonis*
(Linnaeus, 1767)
Adult Size: 350 mm (15 inches)
Depth: Intertidal to over 130 feet
Notes: In coral and rocky areas.
Often seen crossing sand

Family: RANELLIDAE
Common Name: Knobby Triton
Scientific Name:
Cymatium (Gutturnium) muricinum
(Röding, 1798)
Adult Size: 60 mm
Depth: Intertidal to 30 feet
Notes: Among rocks and under stones

Family: RANELLIDAE
Common Name: Reeve's Hairy Triton
Scientific Name:
Cymatium (Monoplex) aquatile
(Wilson, 1993)
Adult Size: 90 mm
Depth: 50 - 100 feet
Notes: In sand and coral rubble

CLASS GASTROPODA

Family: RANELLIDAE
Common Name: Hawaiian Hairy Triton
Scientific Name:
Cymatium (Monoplex) intermedium
Beu & Kay, 1988
Adult Size: 65 mm
Depth: Intertidal to 90 feet
Notes: In tide pools and on shallow reefs

Family: RANELLIDAE
Common Name: Gem Triton
Scientific Name:
Cymatium (Monoplex) mundum
(Gould, 1849)
Adult Size: 38 mm
Depth: 1 - 20 feet
Notes: In tide pools

Family: RANELLIDAE
Common Name: Nicobar Triton
Scientific Name:
Cymatium (Monoplex) nicobaricum
Beu & Kay, 1988
Adult Size: 90 mm
Depth: Intertidal to 300 feet
Notes: Among rocks and under stones

Family: RANELLIDAE
Common Name: Hairy Triton
Scientific Name:
Cymatium (Monoplex) pileare
Wilson, 1993
Adult Size: 85 mm
Depth: 30 - 150 feet
Notes: In rubble

Family: RANELLIDAE
Common Name: Red Triton
Scientific Name:
Cymatium (Septa) rubeculum
(Linnaeus, 1758)
Adult Size: 33 mm
Depth: 15 - 50 feet
Notes: In rubble

Family: RANELLIDAE
Common Name: Wasp Triton
Scientific Name:
Cymatium (Septa) vespaceum
(Lamarck, 1822)
Adult Size: 28 mm
Depth: 60 - 150 feet
Notes: In rubble

CLASS GASTROPODA

Family: RANELLIDAE
Common Name: Large-lipped Triton
Scientific Name:
Cymatium (Turritriton) labiosum
(Wood, 1828)
Adult Size: 25 mm
Depth: 100 - 300 feet
Notes: In rubble

Family: RANELLIDAE
Common Name: Tiny Triton
Scientific Name:
Gyrineum pusillum
(Broderip, 1832)
Adult Size: 17 mm
Depth: Intertidal to 300 feet
Notes: In tidepools and beneath rocks

Family: RANELLIDAE
Common Name: Lesser Girdled Triton
Scientific Name:
Linatella (Gelagna) succincta
(Linnaeus, 1771)
Adult Size: 38 mm
Depth: 35 - 120 feet
Notes: In sand and coral rubble

Family: PERSONIDAE
Common Name: Common Distorsio
Scientific Name: *Distorsio anus*
(Linnaeus, 1758)
Adult Size: 70 mm
Depth: 30 - 80 feet
Notes: In sand pockets and among rocks

Family: PERSONIDAE
Common Name: Burgess' Distorsio (E)
Scientific Name: *Distorsio burgessi*
Lewis, 1972
Adult Size: 40 mm
Depth: 100 - 300 feet
Notes: On rocks

Family: PERSONIDAE
Common Name: Tiny Distorsio
Scientific Name: *Distorsio pusilla*
Pease, 1861
Adult Size: 13 mm
Depth: 30 - 90 feet
Notes: Beneath rocks

CLASS GASTROPODA

CLASS GASTROPODA

BURSIDAE —
Frog Shells

CLASS GASTROPODA

BURSIDAE —
Frog Shells

The knobbed surface of these shells has resulted in the common family name "frog shells" because of the resemblance to the skin of some frogs and toads. Frog shells are characterized by a pronounced canal at the posterior end of the aperture, with some species exhibiting a series of abandoned canals protruding from the right or the left of the shell, all in the same plane. These indicate that frog shells grow in spurts during which a half-turn of new shell is laid down at a time. These growth periods are quiet times when it will find a good hiding place and remain there until the new shell has formed and thickened. Like the tritons, frog shells possess an acid secretion with which they paralyze their prey of various worms. They can be found from tide pools to extremely deep water and are most often heavily encrusted with coralline algae and other organisms, although the inside of the lip remains clean.

Common Name: Warty Frog Shell
Scientific Name: *Bursa bufonia* (Gmelin, 1791)
Adult Size: 92 mm
Depth: 40 - 60 feet
Notes: Beneath rocks

Common Name: Blood-spotted Frog Shell
Scientific Name: *Bursa cruentata* Sowerby, 1841
Adult Size: 41 mm
Depth: 50 - 300 feet
Notes: Beneath rocks

Common Name: Granulate Frog Shell
Scientific Name: *Bursa granularis* (Röding, 1798)
Adult Size: 72 mm
Depth: Intertidal to 80 feet
Notes: In tide pools and beneath rocks

Common Name: Red-mouthed Frog Shell
Scientific Name:
Bursa rhodostoma
Sowerby, 1841
Adult Size: 24 mm
Depth: 45 - 500 feet
Notes: Beneath rocks

Common Name: Wine-mouthed Frog Shell
Scientific Name: *Bursa rosa*
(Perry, 1811)
Adult Size: 46 mm
Depth: Intertidal to 500 feet
Notes: In tide pools and beneath rocks

CLASS GASTROPODA

CLASS GASTROPODA

EULIMIDAE —
Obelisk Shells

CLASS GASTROPODA

EULIMIDAE —
Obelisk Shells

The obelisk shells live in association with echinoderms (sea cucumbers, sea urchins and sea stars) and thus live fairly inactive and protected lives. This lifestyle may explain their lustrous porcelain-like shells. Sea cucumbers seem to be the most favored host and individual sea cucumbers may have more than one species feeding on their tissue at a time. Some obelisk shells may be seen protruding from the skin where they have burrowed beneath the outer layer much like ticks on a dog, or they may live inside the gut of sea cucumbers where one species has taken on a characteristic twist conforming to the convoluted intestine of its host. Species living on sea stars permanently attach themselves to the protected underside where their white shells make them easy for divers to see. Those found on sea urchins also live on the underside of their host, wedged in between the thickened base spines or plates where they are protected, while extending their proboscis into the urchin's skin to feed.

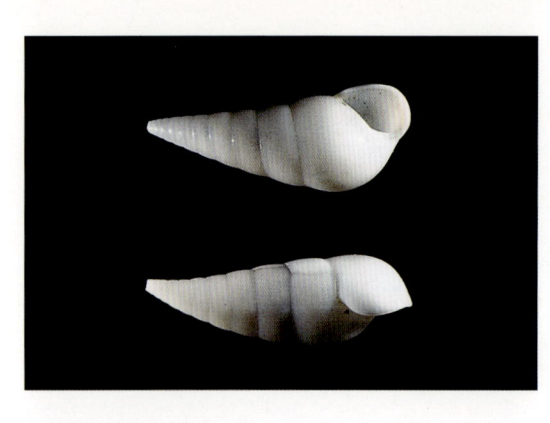

Common Name: Bryan's Obelisk (E)
Scientific Name: *Balcis bryani* (Pilsbry, 1917)
Adult Size: 21 mm
Depth: 60 feet
Notes: Lives on sea cucumbers

Common Name: Thaanum's Obelisk
Scientific Name: *Balcis thaanumi* (Pilsbry, 1917)
Adult Size: 25 mm
Depth: 5 - 10 feet
Notes: Lives in the gut of sea cucumbers

Common Name: Obelisk
Scientific Name: *Balcis* sp.
Adult Size: 20 mm
Depth: 60 feet
Notes: Lives on sea cucumbers

Common Name: Obelisk
Scientific Name: *Balcis* sp.
Adult Size: 28 mm
Depth: 60 feet
Notes: Lives on sea cucumbers

CLASS GASTROPODA

CLASS GASTROPODA

TRIPHORIDAE —
Triphorids

CLASS GASTROPODA

TRIPHORIDAE — Triphorids

The triphorids are an unusual family in that almost all of the members are sinistral, meaning that their shells spiral in a left-handed direction rather than the right-handed (dextral) twist found in almost all other marine shells. The triphorids have a well-developed tubular siphonal canal, a second canal at the posterior end of the aperture, and in many cases a very ornately sculpted shell. The fragile nature of the triphorid shells is practical, because of their relatively protected habitat deep in cracks where they feed on sponges, inaccessible to most predators. They are very common in beach drift, and their shells can be found in almost every handful of sand on protected beaches. In Hawaii they are abundant, and make up a substantial percentage of the micro-shells found in sediments collected around coral reefs.

Common Name: Rival Triphorid
Scientific Name: *Iniforis aemulans* (Hinds, 1843)
Adult Size: 10 mm
Depth: 5 - 300 feet
Notes: Beneath rocks and overhangs. Common in beach sand

Common Name: Harmonious Triphorid
Scientific Name: *Iniforis concors* (Hinds, 1843)
Adult Size: 18 mm
Depth: 5 - 20 feet
Notes: Beneath large rocks and are common in beach sand

Common Name: Glossy Triphorid (E)
Scientific Name: *Iniforis hinuhinu* Kay, 1979
Adult Size: 7 mm
Depth: 30 - 300 feet
Notes: Dead shells are common in sand samples at the bases of ledges

Common Name: Girdled Triphorid
Scientific Name:
Mastonia cingulifera
(Pease, 1861)
Adult Size: 4 mm
Depth: Intertidal to 45 feet
Notes: In tide pools and under rocks in shallow water; dead shells are common in sand samples at the bases of ledges

Common Name: Elongate Triphorid
Scientific Name: *Viriola elongata*
(Laseron, 1958)
Adult Size: 18 mm
Depth: 45 - 200 feet
Notes: Found under rocks at the bases of ledges

Common Name: Incised Triphorid
Scientific Name: *Viriola incisa*
(Pease, 1861)
Adult Size: 13 mm
Depth: 25 - 150 feet
Notes: Found under rocks and at the bases of ledges

CLASS GASTROPODA

Common Name: Pagoda Triphorid
Scientific Name: *Viriola pagoda* (Hinds, 1843)
Adult Size: 27 mm
Depth: 25 feet
Notes: Deep in silt under rubble at the bases of ledges

CLASS GASTROPODA

EPITONIIDAE —
Wentletraps

CLASS GASTROPODA

EPITONIIDAE —
Wentletraps

There is a legend that during the 1800s the precious wentletrap, *Epitonium scalare,* was so highly prized by collectors that paste imitations were made by Chinese craftsmen and sold as the real thing. Today those paste imitations would be worth far more than the real shell, since the shell turned out to be not-so-rare after its habitat was discovered. Wentletraps are generally foraging predators, though some are permanent parasites on corals and anemones. One species can be found living on the undersides of mushroom corals, where it also lays its eggs. They have a wide depth range from tide pools to very deep water. The name wentletrap comes from the Dutch word, "wenteltreppe," meaning spiral stairway, referring to the pronounced ribbing ascending to the apex.

Common Name: Varicose Wentletrap
Scientific Name:
Cirsotrema varicosa
(Lamarck, 1822)
Adult Size: 38 mm
Depth: 10 - 500 feet
Notes: Parasitic on the anemone, *Heteractis malu*

Common Name: Painted Wentletrap
Scientific Name:
Epitonium fucatum
(Pease, 1861)
Adult Size: 31 mm
Depth: Intertidal to 10 feet
Notes: Parasitic on anemones

Common Name: Colored Wentletrap
Scientific Name:
Epitonium replicatum
(Sowerby, 1844)
Adult Size: 14 mm
Depth: 0 - 10 feet
Notes: Sometimes found in beach drift

CLASS GASTROPODA

CLASS GASTROPODA

JANTHINIDAE —
Purple Sea Snails

CLASS GASTROPODA

CLASS GASTROPODA

JANTHINIDAE —
Purple Sea Snails

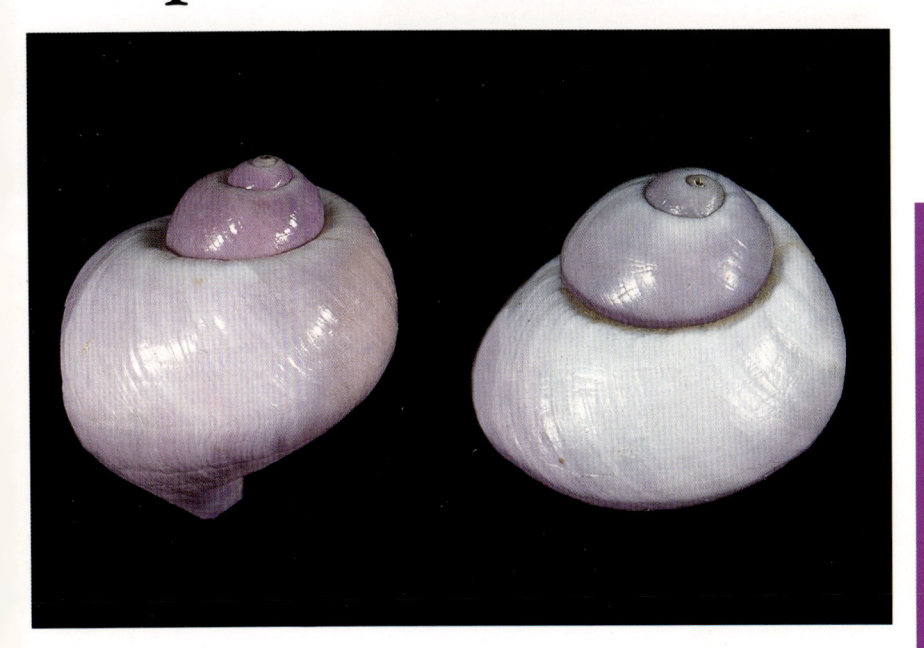

Instead of crawling on the bottom, these snails live their entire adult lives at the surface of the sea. A lightweight shell is buoyed by a float constructed of mucus-covered bubbles. To form the float, the snail extends its foot above the water, capturing a bit of air which it quickly encases in mucus. Many mucus-coated bubbles form the raft. They feed on other organisms which float at the surface, such as Portuguese-man-o-war and by-the-wind sailors. Since they cannot swim, they are entirely dependent on the wind and current to bring them into contact with prey and mates. Fortunately, the bubble raft and the floats and sails of the prey are affected equally by these environmental forces, and so prey is kept nearby.

The unusual lavender color of the shell and animal helps it to blend with the open ocean water, perhaps camouflaging it from fish or birds. At the mercy of wind and waves, these snails are often washed up on beaches after storms.

Common Name: Dwarf Janthina
Scientific Name: *Janthina exigua* Lamarck, 1816
Adult Size: 8 mm
Depth: Surface
Notes: Frequently found in beach drift

Common Name: Globose Janthina
Scientific Name: *Janthina globosa* Swainson, 1822
Adult Size: 24 mm
Depth: Surface
Notes: Frequently found in beach drift

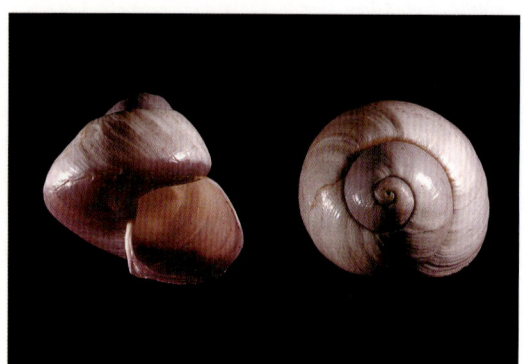

Common Name: Purple Janthina
Scientific Name: *Janthina janthina* (Linnaeus, 1758)
Adult Size: 24 mm
Depth: Surface
Notes: Frequently found in beach drift

CLASS GASTROPODA

MURICIDAE —
Murex Shells

CLASS GASTROPODA

MURICIDAE —
Murex Shells

Of all the seashells, the murexes display the most complexity in shell sculpture and projections. All these spines may discourage predation by fish or other snail-drilling shells, but they also make movement across the bottom complicated. So the animal stretches out, holding the shell high above the bottom, and glides along. Murexes are carnivorous and feed on other seashells, corals, barnacles and echinoderms. They also secrete an acid which aids in boring through shell. The very long end protects the siphon which can poke into places looking for food while remaining protected. The spines can even be used as a wedge to pry open clam shells. In ancient times some species of murex were harvested by the Phoenicians and Egyptians to extract a purple dye used to color cloth.

Common Name: Projecting Murex
Scientific Name: *Aspella producta*
(Pease, 1861)
Adult Size: 18 mm
Depth: Intertidal to 90 feet
Notes: In tide pools and in rubble

Common Name: Hawaiian Burnt Murex (E)
Scientific Name:
Chicoreus insularum
(Pilsbry, 1921)
Adult Size: 110 mm
Depth: 100 - 500 feet
Notes: Forms large aggregations on open sand or on rocks

Common Name: Pele's Murex
Scientific Name:
Homolocantha anatomica
(Perry, 1811)
Adult Size: 60 mm
Depth: 45 - 600 feet
Notes: On rocks and among coral rubble

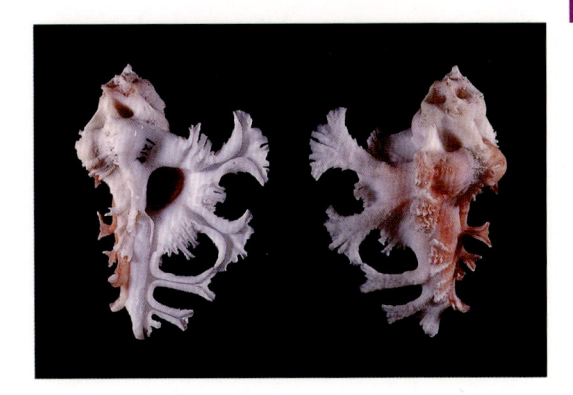

CLASS GASTROPODA

Common Name: Basket Murex
Scientific Name:
Muricodrupa funiculus
(Wood, 1828)
Adult Size: 20 mm
Depth: Intertidal to 10 feet
Notes: Beneath rocks

Common Name: Elongate Murex
Scientific Name:
Pterynotus elongatus
(Solander in Lightfoot, 1786)
Adult Size: 77 mm
Depth: 20 - 60 feet
Notes: On rocks and among coral rubble

Common Name: Three-winged Murex
Scientific Name:
Pterynotus tripterus
(Born, 1778)
Adult Size: 44 mm
Depth: 45 - 60 feet
Notes: In silt among finger coral (*Porites compressa*)

CLASS GASTROPODA

Common Name: Spotted Vitularia
Scientific Name: *Vitularia miliaris*
(Gmelin, 1791)
Adult Size: 35 mm
Depth: 90 - 200 feet
Notes: Associated with black corals

CLASS GASTROPODA

THAIDIDAE —
Rock Shells

CLASS GASTROPODA

THAIDIDAE —
Rock Shells

The rock shells live along rocky shorelines usually exposed to rough water, and thus lack the elaborate projections of other murexes which would only catch the water and make them more likely to be torn from the rock. The top and sides of their shells are often plain and heavily encrusted with coralline algae, making them difficult to distinguish from their background. However, when removed from the rocks, the underside of many species is colorful and lustrous. They, along with the moon shells, are the two best-known groups of shell borers, actually boring a hole through their prey's shell to get at the animal inside. Most of their prey consists of other snails that live on exposed shorelines, such as periwinkles, nerites, limpets and barnacles. Deeper dwellers feed on worms and urchins. They are favored by hermit crabs because their weighty shells are good protection.

Common Name: Mulberry Drupe
Scientific Name:
Drupa (Drupa) morum
Röding, 1798
Adult Size: 30 mm
Depth: Intertidal to 45 feet
Notes: On rocks in high-surge areas

Common Name: Veil Drupe
Scientific Name:
Drupa (Drupa) ricina
(Linnaeus, 1758)
Adult Size: 30 mm
Depth: Intertidal to 45 feet
Notes: In tide pools and on rocks in high-surge areas

Common Name: Strawberry Drupe
Scientific Name:
Drupa (Ricinella) rubusidaeus
Röding, 1798
Adult Size: 38 mm
Depth: Intertidal to 30 feet
Notes: In tide pools and on rocks in high-surge areas

Common Name: Yellow-mouth Drupe
Scientific Name: *Drupella elata* Blainville, 1832
Adult Size: 40 mm
Depth: Intertidal to 10 feet
Notes: In tide pools and on rocks in shallow water

Common Name: Brown Scaly Drupe
Scientific Name: *Morula foliacea* (Conrad, 1837)
Adult Size: 28 mm
Depth: Intertidal to 5 feet
Notes: In tide pools and on reef flats

Common Name: Granulate Drupe
Scientific Name: *Morula granulata* (Duclos, 1832)
Adult Size: 15 mm
Depth: Intertidal to 5 feet
Notes: In tide pools and on rocks in high-surge areas

Common Name: Grape Drupe
Scientific Name: *Morula uva* (Röding, 1798)
Adult Size: 20 mm
Depth: Intertidal to 5 feet
Notes: In tide pools and on reef flats

Common Name: Francolin Rock Shell
Scientific Name: *Nassa serta* (Bruguière, 1789)
Adult Size: 51 mm
Depth: 0 - 40 feet
Notes: Beneath rocks

Common Name: Many-colored Rock Shell
Scientific Name: *Pinaxia versicolor* (Gray, 1839)
Adult Size: 15 mm
Depth: 60 - 350 feet
Notes: Beneath rocks

CLASS GASTROPODA

Common Name: Open Dye Shell
Scientific Name: *Purpura aperta*
(Blainville, 1832)
Adult Size: 70 mm
Depth: Intertidal to 5 feet
Notes: On rocks in high surge areas

Common Name: Intermediate Dye Shell
Scientific Name: *Thais intermedia*
(Kiener, 1836)
Adult Size: 40 mm
Depth: Intertidal 5 feet
Notes: On rocks in high surge areas

Common Name: Flag Rock Shell
Scientific Name: *Vexilla vexillum*
(Gmelin, 1791)
Adult Size: 24 mm
Depth: Intertidal to 5 feet
Notes: Preys on sea urchins

CLASS GASTROPODA

CLASS GASTROPODA

CORALLIOPHILIDAE —
Coral Shells

CLASS GASTROPODA

CORALLIOPHILIDAE —
Coral Shells

Coral shells, as their name suggests, live in close association with corals. Many species live permanently on coral, eating coral tissue and leaving tell-tale scars. Fortunately for these permanent coral-dwellers, many individuals often live on the same coral colony, making potential mates accessible. Some coral shells, like the *Latiaxis,* can be pure white except for their aperture which may have a touch of color within. If these shells lead a protected life, the delicate and lacy sculpturing of the shell remains undamaged. Others like *Coralliophila violacea,* which live a sedentary lifestyle attached to a coral host, can become heavily encrusted with calcium deposits. These deposits can grow so thick that they completely obscure even the shape of the shell. However, the side of the shell attached to the coral remains clean and the lip and aperture are often a deep, shiny purple. The females of this species keep the eggs under their shells until hatching, a habit considered unique within the family Coralliophilidae.

Common Name: Coral Shell
Scientific Name: *Babelomurex* sp.
Adult Size: 23 mm
Depth: 350 feet
Notes: Dredged

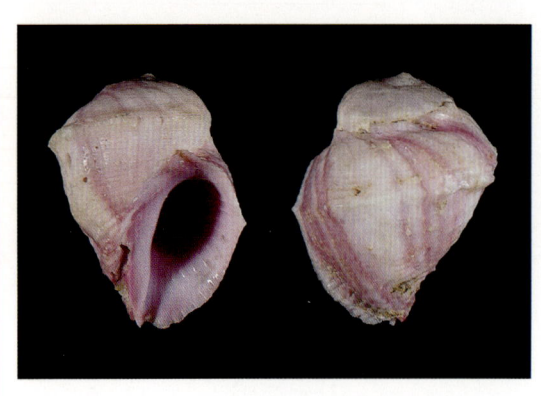

Common Name: Fringed Coral Shell
Scientific Name:
Coralliobia fimbriata
(A. Adams, 1854)
Adult Size: 20 mm
Depth: 10 - 600 feet
Notes: Parasitic on coral

Common Name: Eroded Coral Shell
Scientific Name:
Coralliophila erosa
(Röding, 1798)
Adult Size: 22 mm
Depth: Intertidal to 500 feet
Notes: Parasitic on coral

CLASS GASTROPODA

Common Name: Violet Coral Shell
Scientific Name:
Coralliophila violacea
(Kiener, 1836)
Adult Size: 26 mm
Depth: 50 - 500 feet
Notes: Parasitic on coral

Common Name: Coral Shell
Scientific Name: *Coralliophila* sp.
Adult Size: 20 mm
Depth: 250 feet
Notes: Dredged

Common Name: Coral Shell
Scientific Name: *Coralliophila* sp.
Adult Size: 28 mm
Depth: 1000 feet
Notes: Trawled

CLASS GASTROPODA

Common Name: Coral Shell
Scientific Name: *Hirtomurex* sp.
Adult Size: 27 mm
Depth: 1000 feet
Notes: Trawled

Common Name: Japanese Coral Shell
Scientific Name: *Latiaxis japonicus* (Dunker, 1882)
Adult Size: 47 mm
Depth: 500 - 1000 feet
Notes: Trawled

CLASS GASTROPODA

BUCCINIDAE —
Whelks

CLASS GASTROPODA

BUCCINIDAE —
Whelks

This is a large and diverse family with fusiform shells, a few of which exceed 50 mm. They range from tide pools to great depths and from tropical waters to the Arctic. Though almost all seashells are dextral, or right-hand spiraled, the whelks have several members of their family that have a left-handed, or sinistral, spiral. In some cultures, a left-handed shell is said to bring good luck, and so left-handed species are highly prized. Whelks are active predators which feed on other mollusks and some crustaceans. They are also scavengers and are occasionally attracted to fishermen's traps and hauled up as a byproduct of the day's catch. Some live buried in the sand and others live exposed on the reef flat where their shells become encrusted with other living organisms, obscuring the sculpture and often bright colors of the shells. Most have a thick, brittle operculum which protects the animal when it withdraws into its shell.

Common Name: Flour Whelk
Scientific Name:
Cantharus farinosus
(Gould, 1850)
Adult Size: 14 mm
Depth: 250 - 500 feet
Notes: Dredged

Common Name: Ribbed Whelk
Scientific Name: *Clivipollia costata*
(Pease, 1860)
Adult Size: 23 mm
Depth: 60 - 120 feet
Notes: In finger coral

Common Name: Strawberry Whelk
Scientific Name: *Clivipollia fragaria*
(Wood, 1828)
Adult Size: 23 mm
Depth: 40 - 100 feet
Notes: In finger coral

CLASS GASTROPODA

Common Name: Fiery Whelk
Scientific Name: *Prodotia ignea* (Gmelin, 1791)
Adult Size: 26 mm
Depth: Intertidal to 4 feet
Notes: In tide pools and on shallow reefs

Common Name: Violet-mouth Whelk
Scientific Name: *Prodotia iostomus* (Gray in Griffiths and Pidgeon, 1834)
Adult Size: 28 mm
Depth: 2 - 450 feet
Notes: In rubble

CLASS GASTROPODA

NASSARIIDAE —
Basket Shells

CLASS GASTROPODA

NASSARIIDAE —
Basket Shells

Characteristic of this group is their long siphon which they wave about as they move across the bottom in order to detect prey, which usually consists of decaying animals such as fish and crabs. They also hunt for the source of chemicals given off by living prey such as bivalves. Once these animals have located their prey they are drawn like a magnet with surprising, if not almost frightening, speed. They are so attuned to the scent, that one prey item often attracts many mud snails. As their name suggests, they are mostly shallow water mud- and sand-dwellers. The foot can be used to lash at predators in defense. This activity appears to be designed not so much to hurt the predator as to push the mud snail away. When they are knocked onto their sides, they will thrash around with their foot until they get a purchase in the sand and are able to right themselves. At night they are quite active, and the beauty of the remarkably colorful living animals can be seen as they crawl across the bottom.

Common Name: Burned Basket
Scientific Name:
Nassarius crematus
(Hinds, 1844)
Adult Size: 20 mm
Depth: 60 - 300 feet
Notes: Dredged in sand

Common Name: Gaudy Basket
Scientific Name:
Nassarius gaudiosus
(Hinds, 1844)
Adult Size: 20 mm
Depth: Intertidal to 4 feet
Notes: In tide pools and on shallow reefs

Common Name: Rough Basket
Scientific Name: *Nassarius hirtus*
(Kiener, 1834)
Adult Size: 26 mm
Depth: 40 feet
Notes: In sand

CLASS GASTROPODA

Common Name: Olomea Basket (E)
Scientific Name: *Nassarius olomea* Kay, 1979
Adult Size: 15 mm
Depth: 150 - 300 feet
Notes: Dredged in sand

Common Name: Pimpled Basket
Scientific Name: *Nassarius papillosus* (Linnaeus, 1758)
Adult Size: 40 mm
Depth: 2 - 110 feet
Notes: In sand

CLASS GASTROPODA

FASCIOLARIIDAE —
Spindle Shells

CLASS GASTROPODA

FASCIOLARIIDAE —
Spindle Shells

The living animals of this group are unusually red-pigmented. Some can reach as much as 60 cm and live to great depths. They are ferocious and active carnivores that will climb from beneath the sand during the late afternoon and early evening to search for crabs and other sand-dwelling animals. They move surprisingly quickly along the sand and may cover large areas during their search for food. Waves of fine muscular contractions in the foot propel the snails along. In the trough of the wave the foot is lifted and returned to the bottom a little ahead of the previous position. Many waves of contractions produce a slow, but smooth fluid motion. A thin, smooth layer of horny protein material coats the semi-glossy shell, reducing friction for moving through sand and preventing colonization by encrusting organisms. They lay beautiful, distinctive vase-shaped egg cases.

Common Name: Nicobar Spindle
Scientific Name:
Fusinus nicobaricus
(Röding, 1798)
Adult Size: 200 mm
Depth: 60 - 450 feet
Notes: Half-buried in sand

Common Name: Hawaiian Spindle
Scientific Name:
Fusinus sandvicensis
(Sowerby, 1880)
Adult Size: 110 mm
Depth: 60 - 1000 feet
Notes: In sand

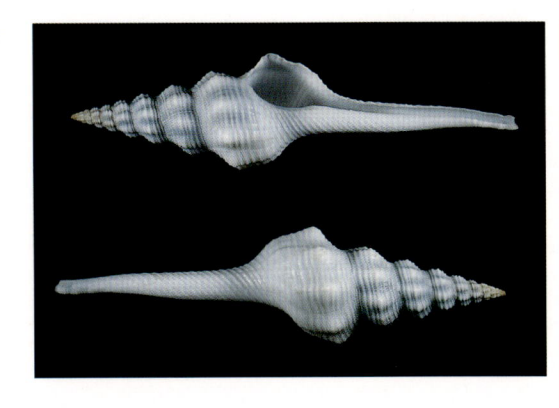

Common Name: Maui Spindle
Scientific Name: *Fusinus* sp.
Adult Size: 150 mm
Depth: 70 feet
Notes: Exposed on sand

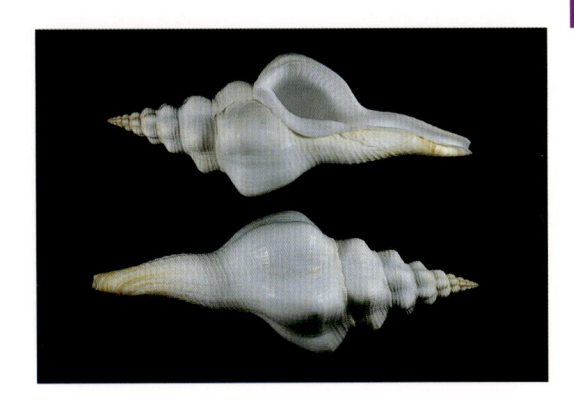

CLASS GASTROPODA

Common Name: Smooth Spindle
Scientific Name: *Fusinus* sp.
Adult Size: 90 mm
Depth: 1000 feet
Notes: Trawled on sand

Common Name: Kurose Spindle
Scientific Name:
Fusolatirus kuroseanus
Okutani, 1975
Adult Size: 40 mm
Depth: 300 - 1000 feet
Notes: Trawled on sand

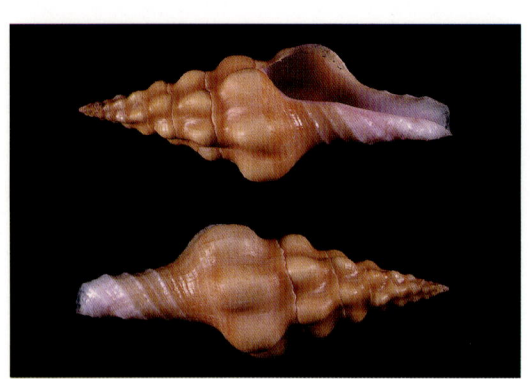

Common Name: Knobby Spindle
Scientific Name: *Latirus nodatus*
(Gmelin, 1791)
Adult Size: 90 mm
Depth: 20 - 80 feet
Notes: Among coral and rocks

CLASS GASTROPODA

Common Name: Gold-banded Spindle
Scientific Name: *Latirus noumeensis* (Crosse, 1870)
Adult Size: 16 mm
Depth: 50 - 150 feet
Notes: In small rubble

Common Name: Banded Spindle
Scientific Name: *Latirulus fasciatus* Habe & Okutani, 1968
Adult Size: 65 mm
Depth: 350 - 1000 feet
Notes: Incidental catch in shrimp trap

Common Name: Green-mouthed Spindle
Scientific Name: *Peristernia chlorostoma* (Sowerby, 1825)
Adult Size: 18 mm
Depth: Intertidal to 4 feet
Notes: Under rocks in tide pools and in shallow water

CLASS GASTROPODA

Common Name: Scaly Spindle
Scientific Name:
Peristernia squamosa
(Pease, 1863)
Adult Size: 18 mm
Depth: 300 - 1000 feet
Notes: Dredged on sand

Common Name: Brown Spindle
Scientific Name:
Peristernia ustulata
(Reeve, 1847)
Adult Size: 24 mm
Depth: 60 - 300 feet
Notes: Dredged on sand

CLASS GASTROPODA

COLUMBELLIDAE —
Dove Shells

CLASS GASTROPODA

COLUMBELLIDAE —
Dove Shells

Although small, most species of dove shells have polished, fusiform shells that are often quite colorful and unusually patterned. Many are so individually variable within the species that they have presented problems for taxonomists, resulting in some confusion, with several names being given to the same species. Not only are they varied in shape and color pattern, but they are also varied in their habits, with many being herbivorous while others are carnivorous, feeding on anemones. Especially active at night, dove shells can be seen most often foraging for food in the evening on sand and among rocks. During the day some are under sand while others can be found clinging to the undersides of rocks in tide pools and down to moderate depths. They can also be found on strands of algae on which they rasp with tiny chitinous teeth. Several species of dove shells, common on Niʻihau and Kauaʻi, have been used to make the most highly prized of all shell necklaces.

Common Name: Miser Dove Shell
Scientific Name: *Anachis miser* (Sowerby, 1844)
Adult Size: 9 mm
Depth: Intertidal to 4 feet
Notes: In tide pools and on reef flats

Common Name: Blue Dove Shell
Scientific Name: *Euplica livescens* (Reeve, 1859)
Adult Size: 12 mm
Depth: unknown
Notes: Beach drift

Common Name: Turtle-dove Dove Shell
Scientific Name: *Euplica turturina* (Lamarck, 1822)
Adult Size: 13 mm
Depth: 60 - 150 feet
Notes: Under rocks

CLASS GASTROPODA

Common Name: Variable Dove Shell
Scientific Name: *Euplica varians* (Sowerby, 1832)
Adult Size: 10 mm
Depth: Intertidal to 4 feet
Notes: Under rocks in tide pools and on shallow reefs

Common Name: Bella Dove Shell
Scientific Name: *Mitrella bella* (Reeve, 1859)
Adult Size: 12 mm
Depth: 60 - 250 feet
Notes: Under rocks

Common Name: Margarite's Dove Shell
Scientific Name: *Mitrella margarita* (Reeve, 1859)
Adult Size: 8 mm
Depth: Intertidal to 300 feet
Notes: In tide pools and beyond the reef

CLASS GASTROPODA

COLUBRARIIDAE —
False Tritons

CLASS GASTROPODA

COLUBRARIIDAE —
False Tritons

This is a very poorly understood family which in the past has been placed with the whelks (Buccinidae) and with the tritons (Cymatiidae), and still lacks a definitive position in the phylogenetic order of mollusks. There is little known about the habits of members of this family. They have been collected alive in sand beneath rocks in relatively shallow water, but there is scant evidence as to what they were doing there. Kay says that: "The minute radula and tiny mouth suggest some form of suctorial feeding with the muscular proboscis wall perhaps used as a pump." The shells are fairly durable and thus commonly found dead or occupied by hermit crabs in tide pools, suggesting a shallow habitat for all three species found in Hawaii.

Common Name: Pointed Serpent
Scientific Name:
Colubraria muricata
(Lightfoot, 1796)
Adult Size: 56 mm
Depth: 40 - 60 feet
Notes: Under rocks, deep in cracks

Common Name: Obscure Serpent
Scientific Name:
Colubraria obscura
(Reeve, 1844)
Adult Size: 33 mm
Depth: Intertidal to 30 feet
Notes: In tide pools and on shallow reefs

Common Name: Twisted Serpent
Scientific Name:
Colubraria tortuosa
(Reeve, 1844)
Adult Size: 46 mm
Depth: Intertidal to 30 feet
Notes: In tide pools and on shallow reefs

CLASS GASTROPODA

CLASS GASTROPODA

OLIVIDAE —
Olive Shells

CLASS GASTROPODA

OLIVIDAE —
Olive Shells

Super-glossy with a distinctive cylindrical shape, olive shells are easily recognized. The shell maintains such gloss in the same manner that cowries do. Two lobes of the mantle fold up over the shell, protecting the glazed surface. The narrow slit opening makes it difficult for a predator such as a crab to get at the animal. Most are sand-dwellers in large numbers and can be found by following their trails just beneath the surface of the sand. The siphon, which is extended above the surface of the sand, allows the olive to detect food on the surface. The olive will then come to the surface, engulf the prey with its foot, smother it in slime and take it under the sand to eat, where other nearby olives may feed on it as well. Olives also search for prey such as other mollusks and small crustaceans underneath the sand. Because they locate prey chemically, eyes are absent or greatly reduced.

Common Name: Hawaiian Olive
Scientific Name:
Oliva paxillus sandwicensis
Pease, 1860
Adult Size: 28 mm
Depth: 30 - 50 feet
Notes: In sand

CLASS GASTROPODA

HARPIDAE —
Harp Shells

CLASS GASTROPODA

HARPIDAE —
Harp Shells

The harp shell family is small with only a couple dozen known species, some of which are very rarely seen. They are characterized by having shells that are heavy, sturdy, glossy and covered with a detailed pattern of rich oranges, browns and maroons. They also have strong radial (top to bottom) ribbing, adding both physical and visual strength to the shell. Harp shells live in sand, silt and mud and are most often encountered just after dark at moderate depths where they come to the surface of the sand to forage for crabs. The harp shell literally pounces on its crab prey in slow motion so as not to alert the crab, enveloping it with its strong muscular foot and then suffocating it by secreting mucus onto the crab's face, incapacitating its gills. This group has the ability to self-amputate the posterior part of the foot to escape predation, much like a lizard may drop its tail when threatened. This may distract the predator long enough for the harp shell to burrow under the sand.

Common Name: Love Harp
Scientific Name: *Harpa amouretta*
Röding, 1798
Adult Size: 34 mm
Depth: 50 - 120 feet
Notes: In sand beneath rubble

Common Name: Goodwin's Harp (E)
Scientific Name: *Harpa goodwini*
Rehder, 1993
Adult Size: 72 mm
Depth: 350 feet
Notes: Crabbed specimens have been taken in lobster traps near Midway

Common Name: Common Harp
Scientific Name: *Harpa major*
Röding, 1798
Adult Size: 83 mm
Depth: 20 - 60 feet
Notes: In sand

Richard L. Goldberg

CLASS GASTROPODA

CLASS GASTROPODA

MITRIDAE —
Miters

CLASS GASTROPODA

MITRIDAE —
Miters

The common family name, miter, has come from the perceived resemblance to a Catholic Bishop's tall, ornamented headdress. Two distinguishing features of this group are the spindle shape and the folds or teeth on the inner lip (columella). They are quite variable and range in size from a few millimeters to over 150 mm, with colors ranging from the spectacular orange of the common *Mitra mitra*, to the usual browns of most sand-dwelling shells. Miters are very diverse in their habitats, being found buried in sand and living among the rocks and corals of the reef. They all possess a long, retractable proboscis which they use to locate food, feeding on everything from worms and clams to detritus. Some will also scavenge the carcasses of dead animals. The larger species are easily found by following a trail in the sand to its end. They are most active at night, but those occupied by hermit crabs are most likely seen by day.

Common Name: Simple Miter
Scientific Name:
Mitra (Mitra) incompta
(Solander in Lightfoot, 1786)
Adult Size: 76 mm
Depth: 20 - 450 feet
Notes: In sand

Common Name: Maui Miter (E)
Scientific Name: *Mitra (Mitra) maui*
Kay, 1979
Adult Size: 37 mm
Depth: 600 - 1000 feet
Notes: Trawled on sand

Common Name: Episcopal Miter
Scientific Name:
Mitra (Mitra) mitra
(Linnaeus, 1758)
Adult Size: 138 mm
Depth: 40 - 400 feet
Notes: In sand

Common Name: Hawaiian Nubila
Scientific Name:
Mitra (Mitra) nubila hawaiiensis
Kay, 1979
Adult Size: 42 mm
Depth: 45 - 120 feet
Notes: In sand within cave entrance

Common Name: Papal Miter
Scientific Name:
Mitra (Mitra) papalis
(Linnaeus, 1758)
Adult Size: 132 mm
Depth: 20 - 150 feet
Notes: In sand channels

Common Name: Pontifical Miter
Scientific Name:
Mitra (Mitra) stictica
(Link, 1807)
Adult Size: 50 mm
Depth: Intertidal to 120 feet
Notes: In sand

CLASS GASTROPODA

Common Name: Dawn Miter
Scientific Name:
Mitra (Nebularia) aurora aurora
Dohrn, 1861
Adult Size: 25 mm
Depth: 5 - 250 feet
Notes: In sand

Common Name: Contracted Miter
Scientific Name:
Mitra (Nebularia) contracta
Swainson, 1820
Adult Size: 38 mm
Depth: 15 - 80 feet
Notes: In sand under rocks

Common Name: Rusty Miter
Scientific Name:
Mitra (Nebularia) ferruginea
Lamarck, 1811
Adult Size: 43 mm
Depth: 60 - 300 feet
Notes: In sand under rubble

Common Name: Strawberry Miter
Scientific Name:
Mitra (Nebularia) fraga
Quoy and Gaimard, 1833
Adult Size: 38 mm
Depth: 80 - 300 feet
Notes: In sand

Common Name: White-mouth Miter
Scientific Name:
Mitra (Nebularia) fulvescens
Broderip, 1836
Adult Size: 34 mm
Depth: 5 - 150 feet
Notes: In sand

CLASS GASTROPODA

Common Name: Inflated Miter
Scientific Name:
Mitra (Nebularia) turgida
Reeve, 1844
Adult Size: 18 mm
Depth: 20 feet
Notes: In sand

Common Name: Black Miter
Scientific Name:
Mitra (Strigatella) assimilis
Pease, 1868
Adult Size: 24 mm
Depth: Intertidal to 5 feet
Notes: In sand under rocks

Common Name: Oily Miter
Scientific Name:
Mitra (Strigatella) fastigium
(Reeve, 1845)
Adult Size: 25 mm
Depth: Intertidal to 4 feet
Notes: In sand in tide pools and on shallow reefs

Common Name: Crenulate Miter
Scientific Name: *Pterygia crenulata*
(Gmelin, 1791)
Adult Size: 32 mm
Depth: Intertidal to 100 feet
Notes: In sand in tide pools and beyond the reef

Common Name: Modest Miter
Scientific Name: *Pterygia pudica*
(Pease, 1860)
Adult Size: 18 mm
Depth: 40 - 240 feet
Notes: In sand and rubble

Common Name: Purtymun's Miter (E)
Scientific Name:
Pterygia purtymuni
Salisbury, 1998
Adult Size: 17 mm
Depth: 20 - 130 feet
Notes: In sand, sometimes associated with pen shell beds

CLASS GASTROPODA

Common Name: Flesh-colored Miter
Scientific Name:
Cancilla (Domiporta)
sp. cf. *carnicolor*
(Reeve, 1844)
Adult Size: 20 mm
Depth: 65 - 600 feet
Notes: In sand

Common Name: Granite Miter
Scientific Name:
Cancilla (Domiporta) granatina
(Lamarck, 1811)
Adult Size: 38 mm
Depth: 40 - 1500 feet
Notes: In sand

Common Name: Olive-shaped Miter
Scientific Name:
Imbricaria olivaeformis
(Swainson, 1821)
Adult Size: 17 mm
Depth: 30 - 240 feet
Notes: In sand

Common Name: Emerson's Miter
Scientific Name:
Neocancilla clathrus
(Gmelin, 1791)
Adult Size: 32 mm
Depth: 20 - 150 feet
Notes: In sand

Common Name: Langford's Miter
Scientific Name:
Neocancilla papilio langfordiana
J. Cate, 1962
Adult Size: 28 mm
Depth: 30 - 350 feet
Notes: In sand

Common Name: Newcomb's Miter (E)
Scientific Name:
Scabricola (Swainsonia) newcombii
(Pease, 1869)
Adult Size: 37 mm
Depth: 30 - 300 feet
Notes: In sand

Common Name: Warty Miter
Scientific Name:
Subcancilla verrucosa
(Reeve, 1845)
Adult Size: 27 mm
Depth: 100 - 600 feet
Notes: In sand

CLASS GASTROPODA

CLASS GASTROPODA

COSTELLARIIDAE —
Ribbed Miters

CLASS GASTROPODA

COSTELLARIIDAE —
Ribbed Miters

These are among the most elegantly colored and shaped of all the miters. Their distinguishing feature is a series of finely sculptured cords which begin at the outer lip and extend down into the aperture. Like all miters they are predatory, living their entire lives buried in sand where they hunt their prey of worms and small mollusks. An extremely long and flexible proboscis may be as long as the shell. With it they inject venom into the prey and then consume the prey after it is paralyzed. They can occasionally be seen on the surface of the sand at night when they are more actively hunting. They are preyed on by rays that fan the sand with their wings, sending the hapless miters tumbling. The ray then sucks them into its mouth where they are crunched up by its hard teeth and powerful jaws. Generally just the animal is eaten by the ray and the broken shell drops back to the bottom where pieces are often found by divers. They are also found drilled by other mollusks.

Common Name: War Miter
Scientific Name:
Vexillum (Costellaria) bellum
(Pease, 1860)
Adult Size: 25 mm
Depth: 20 to 300 feet
Notes: In sand and rubble

Common Name: Basket Miter
Scientific Name:
Vexillum (Costellaria) corbiculum
(Sowerby, 1870)
Adult Size: 19 mm
Depth: 45 - 180 feet
Notes: In sand and rubble

Common Name: Thaanum's Miter
Scientific Name:
Vexillum (Costellaria) interstriatum
(Sowerby, 1870)
Adult Size: 28 mm
Depth: 20 - 300 feet
Notes: In sand

Common Name: Moana Miter
Scientific Name:
Vexillum (Costellaria) leucozonias
Deshayes in La Borde and Linant,
1834
Adult Size: 14 mm
Depth: 45 - 300 feet
Notes: In sand

Common Name: Pacific Miter
Scientific Name:
Vexillum (Costellaria) pacificum
(Reeve, 1845)
Adult Size: 25 mm
Depth: 40 - 250 feet
Notes: In sand

Common Name: One-banded Miter
Scientific Name:
Vexillum (Costellaria) unifasciatum
(Wood, 1828)
Adult Size: 25 mm
Depth: 40 - 60 feet
Notes: In sand

CLASS GASTROPODA

Common Name: Wolfe's Miter
Scientific Name:
Vexillum (Costellaria) wolfei
Cernohorsky, 1978
Adult Size: 12 mm
Depth: 150 - 300 feet
Notes: Dredged in sand

Common Name: Approximate Miter
Scientific Name:
Vexillum (Pusia) approximatum
(Pease, 1860)
Adult Size: 20 mm
Depth: 35 - 90 feet
Notes: In sand

Common Name: Nodose Miter
Scientific Name:
Vexillum (Pusia) cancellarioides
(Anton, 1839)
Adult Size: 15 mm
Depth: Intertidal to 20 feet
Notes: On rocks in high-surge areas

Common Name: Chain Miter
Scientific Name:
Vexillum (Pusia) catenatum
(Broderip, 1836)
Adult Size: 18 mm
Depth: 70 - 90 feet
Notes: In sand

Common Name: Cuming's Miter
Scientific Name:
Vexillum (Pusia) cumingii
(Reeve, 1844)
Adult Size: 27 mm
Depth: 20 - 80 feet
Notes: In sand

Common Name: Elegant Miter
Scientific Name:
Vexillum (Pusia) lautum
(Reeve, 1845)
Adult Size: 14 mm
Depth: Intertidal to 60 feet
Notes: Under rocks in tide pools and on shallow reefs

CLASS GASTROPODA

Common Name: Fiery Miter
Scientific Name:
Vexillum (Pusia) moelleri
(Kuster, 1840)
Adult Size: 20 mm
Depth: 45 - 60 feet
Notes: In sand and rubble

Common Name: Tuberose Miter
Scientific Name:
Vexillum (Pusia) tuberosum
(Reeve, 1845)
Adult Size: 13 mm
Depth: Intertidal to 300 feet
Notes: In sand

Common Name: Halo Miter
Scientific Name:
Vexillum (Pusia) unifascialis
(Lamarck, 1811)
Adult Size: 16 mm
Depth: 30 - 60 feet
Notes: In sand

CLASS GASTROPODA

TURRIDAE/CLAVINIDAE —
Turrids

CLASS GASTROPODA

TURRIDAE/CLAVINIDAE —
Turrids

While there is no characteristic turrid shape, they do share one very curious characteristic. They all have a notch or slit on the outside of the lip of the shell much like that seen in the strombs, except thinner. It may run deeply into the shell's lip or be barely visible. Turrids are by far the largest family group among the seashells and also one of the oldest, represented in the fossil record as long ago as 135 million years during the Cretaceous. During this long presence on Earth they have occupied every geographic locality from the poles to the tropics and an amazing range of habitats from tide pools to the depths of the ocean. They may live in sand or under rocks. Though many are very small (2 to 10 mm), some, such as one specimen from Japanese waters, can reach 160 mm. They feed on a variety of foods, either engulfing or stinging their prey. Some have a venomous harpoon similar to that of the cone shells, with which they spear and immobilize their prey.

Family: TURRIDAE
Common Name: Polished Turrid
Scientific Name:
Gemmula interpolata
Powell, 1967
Adult Size: 55 mm
Depth: 120 - 2000 feet
Notes: Trawled on sand

Family: TURRIDAE
Common Name: Necklace Turrid
Scientific Name:
Gemmula monilifera
(Pease, 1861)
Adult Size: 25 mm
Depth: 20 - 600 feet
Notes: In sand

Family: TURRIDAE
Common Name: False Necklace Turrid
Scientific Name:
Gemmula pseudomonilifera
Powell, 1967
Adult Size: 23 mm
Depth: 45 - 50 feet
Notes: In sand

CLASS GASTROPODA

Family: TURRIDAE
Common Name: Crested Turrid
Scientific Name:
Turridrupa bijubata
(Reeve, 1843)
Adult Size: 16 mm
Depth: 60 - 150 feet
Notes: In sand and rubble

Family: TURRIDAE
Common Name: Related Turrid
Scientific Name:
Turridrupa consobrina
Powell, 1967
Adult Size: 17 mm
Depth: 45 feet
Notes: In sand

Family: TURRIDAE
Common Name: Weaver's Turrid
Scientific Name:
Turridrupa weaveri
Powell, 1967
Adult Size: 25 mm
Depth: 40 - 1000 feet
Notes: In silt beneath rubble

Family: TURRIDAE
Common Name: Brown Turrid
Scientific Name:
Xenoturris castanella
Powell, 1964
Adult Size: 23 mm
Depth: 45 - 120 feet
Notes: In sand

Family: TURRIDAE
Common Name: Horn-shaped Turrid
Scientific Name:
Xenoturris cerithiformis
Powell, 1964
Adult Size: 48 mm
Depth: 30 - 300 feet
Notes: In sand

Family: TURRIDAE
Common Name: King's Turrid
Scientific Name: *Xenoturris kingae*
Powell, 1964
Adult Size: 25 mm
Depth: 30 - 600 feet
Notes: In sand

CLASS GASTROPODA

Family: CLAVINIDAE
Common Name: Knobbed Turrid
Scientific Name:
Clavus (Spendrillia) nodifera
(Pease, 1860)
Adult Size: 16 mm
Depth: 60 feet
Notes: In sand and rubble

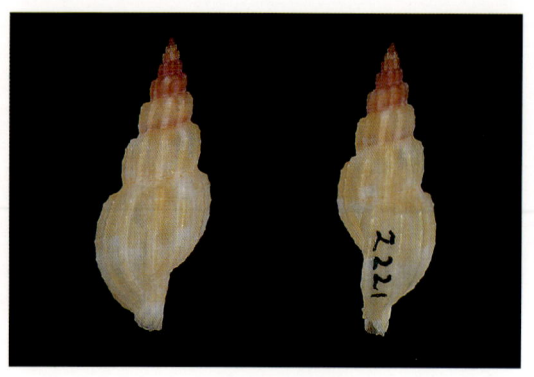

Family: CLAVINIDAE
Common Name: Cuming's Turrid
Scientific Name:
Tritonoturris cumingii
(Powys, 1835)
Adult Size: 18 mm
Depth: 60 feet
Notes: In rubble and sand

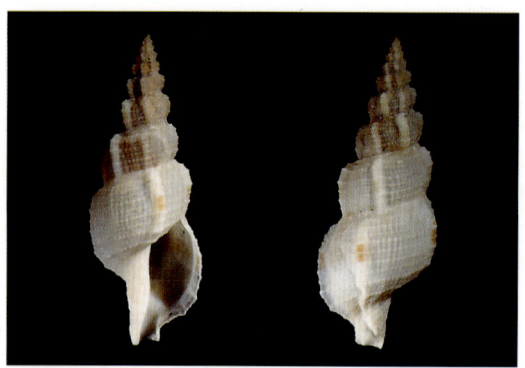

Family: CLAVINIDAE
Common Name: Robillard's Turrid
Scientific Name:
Tritonoturris robillardi
(H. Adams, 1869)
Adult Size: 27 mm
Depth: 60 - 80 feet
Notes: In rubble

CLASS GASTROPODA

CONIDAE —
Cone Shells

CLASS GASTROPODA

CONIDAE —
Cone Shells

The cone shell family contains some very beautiful and colorfully-patterned members with a distinctive, easily recognized shape. They are specialized feeders feeding on worms, mollusks or small fish. All cones have venom glands and they are capable of reaching all parts of their shell to defend themselves against octopus or carnivorous mollusks. But the primarily use of the venom is to immobilize prey. The barbed teeth, which look like arrows, are released when a worm or snail is fired upon, but when the intended prey is a fish which could swim away, the tooth is held onto by the cone shell until the venom takes effect. These teeth can be 10 - 20 mm in the large fish-eating species such as *Conus striatus!* While there are many shell-eating fish, cones are the only shells which are known to strike back. The siphon extends above the surface of the sand sensing a fish above. Then the proboscis moves up to the surface of the sand and fires a venom-filled tooth into the fish. The venom affects the nervous system causing lack of muscular coordination and eventually respiratory failure. The cone then rears up above the sand and engulfs the fish whole. The same symptoms occur whether the victim is a worm or a human. Some large cones are capable of killing a person within five minutes. Less serious symptoms include paralysis and intense pain.

Cone shells are found in all habitats from shallow to moderate depths. The sand-dwelling species possess very clean shells, while those that live out on top of the sand or among rocks or rubble have shells whose pattern is obscured by a layer called the periostracum. Resembling thin brown moss in some species, this layer prevents organisms from growing on the shell and helps to camouflage it. Most are crepuscular (active at twilight or just before dawn) or nocturnal. Certain hermit crabs are especially adapted to living within the very narrow opening of a dead cone shell. The bodies of these crabs are flattened compared to other types of hermit crabs.

Common Name: Abbreviated Cone (E)
Scientific Name:
Conus abbreviatus
Reeve, 1843
Adult Size: 35 mm
Depth: Intertidal to 20 feet
Notes: In sand in tide pools and in shallow water

Common Name: Pointed Cone
Scientific Name:
Conus acutangulus
Lamarck, 1811
Adult Size: 22 mm
Depth: 70 - 180 feet
Notes: In sand

Common Name: Banded Cone
Scientific Name: *Conus bandanus*
Hwass, in Bruguière, 1792
Adult Size: 132 mm
Depth: 15 - 300 feet
Notes: On sand

Common Name: Bubble Cone
Scientific Name: *Conus bullatus*
Linnaeus, 1758
Adult Size: 55 mm
Depth: 60 - 200 feet
Notes: Beneath sand where the bottom is covered with coralline algae nodules

Common Name: Cat Cone
Scientific Name: *Conus catus*
Hwass in Bruguière, 1792
Adult Size: 39 mm
Depth: Intertidal to 30 feet
Notes: In sand on reef flats and in shallow water

Common Name: Chaldean Cone
Scientific Name: *Conus chaldeus*
(Röding, 1798)
Adult Size: 27 mm
Depth: Intertidal to 5 feet
Notes: In tide pools and on reef flats

CLASS GASTROPODA

Common Name: Circumactus Cone
Scientific Name:
Conus circumactus
Iredale, 1929
Adult Size: 57 mm
Depth: 40 - 350 feet
Notes: In sand and rubble

Common Name: Spicer's Cone
Scientific Name:
Conus coelinae spiceri
Bartsch & Rehder, 1943
Adult Size: 110 mm
Depth: 40 - 70 feet
Notes: On sand

Common Name: Distant Cone
Scientific Name: *Conus distans*
Hwass in Bruguière, 1792
Adult Size: 85 mm
Depth: 6 - 30 feet
Notes: On hard substrate with thin layer of sand

Common Name: Hebrew Cone
Scientific Name: *Conus ebraeus*
Linnaeus, 1758
Adult Size: 45 mm
Depth: 2 - 40 feet
Notes: In sand or exposed on reef flats and shallow reefs

Common Name: Literary Cone (E)
Scientific Name:
Conus eugrammatus
Bartsch and Rehder, 1943
Adult Size: 35 mm
Depth: 200 - 1000 feet
Notes: Trawled in sand

Common Name: Yellow Cone
Scientific Name: *Conus flavidus*
Lamarck, 1810
Adult Size: 46 mm
Depth: 2 - 10 feet
Notes: In sand on reef flat

CLASS GASTROPODA

Common Name: Imperial Cone
Scientific Name: *Conus imperialis* Linnaeus, 1758
Adult Size: 70 mm
Depth: 50 to 180 feet
Notes: Among coral and rocks

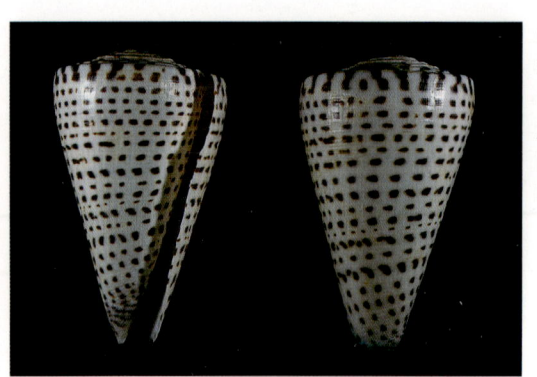

Common Name: Leopard Cone
Scientific Name: *Conus leopardus* (Röding, 1798)
Adult Size: 150 mm
Depth: 5 - 150 feet
Notes: On sand

Common Name: Scripted Cone
Scientific Name: *Conus litoglyphus* Hwass in Bruguière, 1792
Adult Size: 40 mm
Depth: 30 - 200 feet
Notes: In sand

Common Name: Livid Cone
Scientific Name: *Conus lividus*
Hwass in Bruguière, 1792
Adult Size: 52 mm
Depth: 10 - 30 feet
Notes: On reef flats and shallow reefs

Common Name: Soldier Cone
Scientific Name: *Conus miles*
Linnaeus, 1758
Adult Size: 65 mm
Depth: 45 - 90 feet
Notes: On reef flats and shallow reefs

Common Name: Morelet's Cone
Scientific Name: *Conus moreleti*
Crosse, 1858
Adult Size: 52 mm
Depth: 20 - 60 feet
Notes: In sand and rubble

CLASS GASTROPODA

Common Name: Nussatella Cone
Scientific Name: *Conus nussatella* Linnaeus, 1758
Adult Size: 47 mm
Depth: 50 - 70 feet
Notes: In silt among finger coral

Common Name: Obscure Cone
Scientific Name: *Conus obscurus* Sowerby, 1833
Adult Size: 35 mm
Depth: 50 - 150 feet
Notes: Under rocks

Common Name: Arrow Cone
Scientific Name: *Conus pennaceus* Born, 1780
Adult Size: 55 mm
Depth: 10 - 30 feet
Notes: In sand pockets on reef flats and in shallow water

Common Name: Perforated Cone
Scientific Name: *Conus pertusus*
Hwass in Bruguière, 1792
Adult Size: 30 mm
Depth: 50 - 200 feet
Notes: In sand under rocks

Common Name: Calf Cone
Scientific Name: *Conus planorbis*
Born, 1778
Adult Size: 55 mm
Depth: 50 - 60 feet
Notes: On sand

Common Name: Flea Cone
Scientific Name: *Conus pulicarius*
Hwass in Bruguière, 1792
Adult Size: 60 mm
Depth: 40 - 200 feet
Notes: On and under sand on reef flats and beyond the reef

CLASS GASTROPODA

Common Name: Oak Cone
Scientific Name: *Conus quercinus*
Lightfoot, 1786
Adult Size: 110 mm
Depth: 10 - 250 feet
Notes: On sand

Common Name: Rat Cone
Scientific Name: *Conus rattus*
Hwass in Bruguière, 1792
Adult Size: 52 mm
Depth: 2 - 20 feet
Notes: On reef flats and shallow reefs

Common Name: Retiform Cone
Scientific Name: *Conus retifer*
Menke, 1829
Adult Size: 46 mm
Depth: 40 - 60 feet
Notes: In sand

Common Name: Sazanka's Cone
Scientific Name: *Conus sazanka*
Shikama, 1970
Adult Size: 20 mm
Depth: 300 feet
Notes: In sand

Common Name: Marriage Cone
Scientific Name: *Conus sponsalis*
Hwass in Bruguière, 1792
Adult Size: 30 mm
Depth: Intertidal to 300 feet
Notes: On reef flat

Common Name: Striated Cone
Scientific Name: *Conus striatus*
Linnaeus, 1758
Adult Size: 108 mm
Depth: 20 - 50 feet
Notes: In sand beneath rocks

CLASS GASTROPODA

Common Name: Sutured Cone
Scientific Name: *Conus suturatus sandwichensis* Reeve, 1844
Adult Size: 48 mm
Depth: 110 - 500 feet
Notes: On sand

Common Name: Textile Cone
Scientific Name: *Conus textile* Linnaeus, 1758
Adult Size: 124 mm
Depth: 5 - 120 feet
Notes: In sand beneath coral

Common Name: Flag Cone
Scientific Name: *Conus vexillum* Gmelin, 1791
Adult Size: 120 mm
Depth: 40 - 150 feet
Notes: On sand

CLASS GASTROPODA

CLASS GASTROPODA

TEREBRIDAE —
Augers

CLASS GASTROPODA

TEREBRIDAE —
Augers

Augers often give away their presence by the furrow created as they plow through sand. While intuitively it would seem that the pointed end leads the way, it is the wider end, where the animal protrudes, which pulls the shell through the sand. Augers are carnivorous and feed on various types of sand-dwelling worms. Some engulf their prey whole and some have a venom gland to rapidly immobilize the worm. During the day, when augers are beneath the sand, a siphon extends to the surface of the sand so that the snail can "breathe" and wastes can be excreted. Augers can withdraw far enough into their shells that crabs and fish often are unable to reach them. Some crabs and predators such as eagle rays, however, are capable of crushing the shell. Occasionally they succeed only in snapping off the pointed end, and still cannot get to the animal inside. Other predatory snails are capable of drilling a hole through the shell to get at the animal.

Common Name: Gould's Auger (E)
Scientific Name: *Duplicaria gouldi*
Deshayes, 1859
Adult Size: 65 mm
Depth: 2 - 300 feet
Notes: In sand

Common Name: Thaanum's Auger (E)
Scientific Name:
Duplicaria thaanumi
(Pilsbry, 1921)
Adult Size: 70 mm
Depth: 40 - 250 feet
Notes: In sand

Common Name: Hectic Auger
Scientific Name: *Hastula hectica*
(Linnaeus, 1758)
Adult Size: 45 mm
Depth: Supratidal to 2 feet
Notes: In sand on beaches. Often exposed by receding waves

CLASS GASTROPODA

Common Name: Inconstant Auger (E)
Scientific Name: *Hastula inconstans* (Hinds, 1844)
Adult Size: 32 mm
Depth: 10 - 20 feet
Notes: In sand

Common Name: Lance Auger
Scientific Name: *Hastula lanceata* (Linnaeus, 1758)
Adult Size: 44 mm
Depth: 10 - 300 feet
Notes: In sand

Common Name: Praised Auger
Scientific Name: *Hastula matheroniana* (Deshayes, 1859)
Adult Size: 23 mm
Depth: 15 - 300 feet
Notes: In sand

Common Name: Pencil Auger
Scientific Name: *Hastula penicillata*
(Hinds, 1844)
Adult Size: 28 mm
Depth: 5 - 50 feet
Notes: In sand

Common Name: Lead Auger
Scientific Name: *Hastula plumbea*
Quoy & Gaimard, 1833
Adult Size: 17 mm
Depth: 20 - 450 feet
Notes: In sand

Common Name: Verreaux's Auger
Scientific Name: *Hastula strigilata*
(Linnaeus, 1758)
Adult Size: 38 mm
Depth: 30 - 300 feet
Notes: In sand

CLASS GASTROPODA

Common Name: Agate Auger
Scientific Name: *Terebra achates*
Weaver, 1960
Adult Size: 132 mm
Depth: 10 - 300 feet
Notes: In sand

Common Name: Similar Auger
Scientific Name: *Terebra affinis*
Gray, 1834
Adult Size: 45 mm
Depth: 5 - 600 feet
Notes: In sand

Common Name: White Auger
Scientific Name: *Terebra albula*
(Menke, 1843)
Adult Size: 18 mm
Depth: 2 - 200 feet
Notes: In sand

Common Name: Amanda's Auger
Scientific Name: *Terebra amanda*
Hinds, 1844
Adult Size: 27 mm
Depth: 30 - 60 feet
Notes: In sand

Common Name: Pleasant Auger
Scientific Name: *Terebra amoena*
Deshayes, 1859
Adult Size: 55 mm
Depth: 120 feet
Notes: In sand

Common Name: Dark-spotted Auger
Scientific Name: *Terebra areolata* (Link, 1807)
Adult Size: 148 mm
Depth: 5 - 70 feet
Notes: In sand

CLASS GASTROPODA

Common Name: Short-whorled Auger
Scientific Name:
Terebra argus brachygyra
Pilsbry 1921
Adult Size: 70 mm
Depth: 30 - 40 feet
Notes: In sand

Common Name: Babylon Auger
Scientific Name: *Terebra babylonia*
Lamarck, 1822
Adult Size: 42 mm
Depth: 5 - 600 feet
Notes: In sand

Common Name: Spalding's Auger
Scientific Name: *Terebra cerithina*
Lamarck, 1822
Adult Size: 25 mm
Depth: 30 - 50 feet
Notes: In sand

Common Name: Yellow Auger
Scientific Name: *Terebra chlorata*
Lamarck, 1822
Adult Size: 60 mm
Depth: 40 - 60 feet
Notes: In sand

Common Name: Column Auger
Scientific Name:
Terebra columellaris
Hinds, 1844
Adult Size: 40 mm
Depth: 30 - 600 feet
Notes: In sand

Common Name: Crenulate Auger
Scientific Name: *Terebra crenulata*
(Linnaeus, 1758)
Adult Size: 87 mm
Depth: 2 - 300 feet
Notes: In sand

CLASS GASTROPODA

Common Name: Divided Auger
Scientific Name: *Terebra dimidiata*
(Linnaeus, 1758)
Adult Size: 100 mm
Depth: 3 - 5 feet
Notes: In sand

Common Name: Tiger Auger
Scientific Name: *Terebra felina*
(Dillwyn, 1817)
Adult Size: 67 mm
Depth: 30 - 40 feet
Notes: In sand

Common Name: Yellow-banded Auger
Scientific Name:
Terebra flavofasciata
Pilsbry, 1921
Adult Size: 45 mm
Depth: 10 - 500 feet
Notes: In sand

CLASS GASTROPODA

Common Name: Funnel Auger
Scientific Name: *Terebra funiculata*
Hinds, 1844
Adult Size: 35 mm
Depth: 10 - 600 feet
Notes: In sand

Common Name: White-spotted Auger
Scientific Name: *Terebra guttata* (Röding, 1798)
Adult Size: 95 mm
Depth: 5 - 80 feet
Notes: In sand

Common Name: Kilburn's Auger
Scientific Name: *Terebra kilburni*
Burch, 1965
Adult Size: 37 mm
Depth: 300 feet
Notes: Dredged in sand

CLASS GASTROPODA

Common Name: Marlinspike Auger
Scientific Name: *Terebra maculata* (Linnaeus, 1758)
Adult Size: 230 mm
Depth: 2 - 600 feet
Notes: In sand.

Common Name: Red-cloud Auger
Scientific Name: *Terebra nebulosa* Sowerby, 1825
Adult Size: 32 mm
Depth: 10 - 30 feet
Notes: In sand

Common Name: Shiny Auger
Scientific Name: *Terebra nitida* Hinds, 1844
Adult Size: 24 mm
Depth: 45 - 450 feet
Notes: In sand

CLASS GASTROPODA

Common Name: Perforated Auger
Scientific Name: *Terebra pertusa*
(Born, 1778)
Adult Size: 53 mm
Depth: 35 - 500 feet
Notes: In sand

Common Name: Virgin Auger
Scientific Name: *Terebra virgo*
Schepman, 1913
Adult Size: 22 mm
Depth: 250 feet
Notes: In sand

Common Name: Pygmy Auger
Scientific Name:
Terenolla pygmaea
(Hinds, 1844)
Adult Size: 15 mm
Depth: 5 - 60 feet
Notes: In sand

CLASS GASTROPODA

CLASS GASTROPODA

ARCHITECTONICIDAE —
Sundials

CLASS GASTROPODA

ARCHITECTONICIDAE —
Sundials

The name of this family comes from the Greek word architekton, which means master-builder, in reference to the beautiful construction of these shells. These finely detailed snails remain clean and glossy because they are sand-dwellers, a behavior which prevents other organisms from fouling the shell. They come out only at night and feed on corals and sea anemones, but can sometimes be seen by wading in shallow water among sea grass in the evening and looking for their distinctive round coiling shape. The small beads of the spiraling underside and the deep umbilicus resemble a miniature circular staircase and sometimes juvenile sundials can be found up inside this umbilicus! Though not always easy to find, they are one of the most common shells in shell markets where they are sold by the basket-full at very low prices.

Common Name: Clear Sundial
Scientific Name:
Architectonica perspectiva
(Linnaeus, 1758)
Adult Size: 32 mm
Depth: 90 -150 feet
Notes: In sand

Common Name: Sterk's Sundial
Scientific Name: *Heliacus sterkii*
(Pilsbry & Vanatta, 1908)
Adult Size: 7 mm
Depth: 10 - 300 feet
Notes: In sand

Common Name: Variegated Sundial
Scientific Name:
Heliacus variegatus
(Gmelin, 1791)
Adult Size: 15 mm
Depth: 2 - 4 feet
Notes: In sand

Common Name: Eight-keeled Sundial
Scientific Name: *Philippia oxytropis*
A. Adams, 1855
Adult Size: 16 mm
Depth: 2 - 200 feet
Notes: In sand

Common Name: Radiating Sundial
Scientific Name: *Philippia radiata*
(Röding, 1798)
Adult Size: 16 mm
Depth: 2 - 150 feet
Notes: In sand

CLASS GASTROPODA

38 *PYRAMIDELLIDAE* —
Pyramid Shells

CLASS GASTROPODA

38   PYRAMIDELLIDAE —
Pyramid Shells

Pyramidellids and one other group, the Cephalaspids (including the pupas and bubble shells), are the only shelled members of the opisthobranchs to have a spiral shell. All other members of this group have reduced or simplified shells. Because they have retained the spiral shell, but have other physiological characteristics of opisthobranchs, they are considered to be the earliest-evolved of the opisthobranchs. Unlike the Cephalaspids, the Pyramidellids have straight-sided shells with a high spire. They prefer shallow, protected water where they are often ectoparasites on polychaete worms, bivalves and gastropods from which they suck the blood using a specialized pumping pharynx. They may be found in relative abundance in harbors and bays where they leave trails on the silty sand or mud bottom. They are most active at night and can be seen exposed on the substrate.

Common Name: Hatchet Pyramid
Scientific Name:
Pyramidella dolabrata
(Linnaeus, 1758)
Adult Size: 26 mm
Depth: 10 - 45 feet
Notes: In sand

Common Name: Furrow Pyramid
Scientific Name:
Pyramidella sulcata
A. Adams, 1854
Adult Size: 28 mm
Depth: 40 - 300 feet
Notes: In sand

Common Name: Cornellian Pyramid
Scientific Name:
Turbonilla cornelliana
(Newcomb, 1870)
Adult Size: 23 mm
Depth: 20 - 300 feet
Notes: In sand

CLASS GASTROPODA

ACTAEONIDAE/BULLINIDAE —
Pupa Shells and Bullinids

CLASS GASTROPODA

ACTAEONIDAE/BULLINIDAE —
Pupa Shells and Bullinids

Members of the Actaeonidae are the most primitive in the order Cephalaspidea. They differ from more advanced members of the order in possessing a well-calcified shell, a well-defined spire and an aperture that does not extend the entire length of the body whorl. A small operculum is sometimes even present. While the shells of more advanced groups are white or transparent, pupa shells can be somewhat colorful. They possess a spatulate-shape head which aids in burrowing beneath sand. Some Hawaiian pupa shells have been found in relatively deep water on open sand scattered with small rubble or the calcified "leaves" of *Halimeda* algae. In shallow water they live under sand by day, feeding on polychaete worms, and emerge at night. The Bullinids also possess heavily calcified shells and live under sand by day.

Family: ACTAEONIDAE
Pupas
Common Name: Modest Pupa
Scientific Name: *Pupa pudica*
(A. Adams, 1854)
Adult Size: 12 mm
Depth: 120 - 350 feet
Notes: Dredged in sand

Family: ACTAEONIDAE
Pupas
Common Name: Tessellate Pupa
Scientific Name: *Pupa tessellata*
(Reeve, 1842)
Adult Size: 15 mm
Depth: 10 - 120 feet
Notes: In sand

Family: BULLINIDAE **Bullinids**
Common Name: Lined Bubble
Scientific Name: *Bullina lineata*
(Gray, 1825)
Adult Size: 8 mm
Depth: 1 - 2 feet
Notes: In sand

CLASS GASTROPODA

CLASS GASTROPODA

HYDATINIDAE — Paper Bubbles
CYLICHNIDAE — Cylindrical Bubbles
HAMINOEIDAE — White Bubbles
BULLIDAE — True Bubbles

CLASS GASTROPODA

HYDATINIDAE — Paper Bubbles
CYLICHNIDAE — Cylindrical Bubbles
HAMINOEIDAE — White Bubbles
BULLIDAE — True Bubbles

The four families above possess delicate shells with an extremely inflated body whorl and an almost flat or sunken spire. Like the pupa shells, most feed on polychaete worms and are found in relatively protected sand environments. They are common in tide pools, in crevices and under rocks in the shallow water shoreward of the fringing reef where there is little or moderate wave action, on sand bottom in bays not affected by current, and on sand bottom in deep water. All three of these habitats have fairly stable water conditions, only rarely affected by storms. Most species are seen out at night, often in numbers. Although the first three families covered here are carnivorous, the Bullidae are herbivores.

Family: HYDATINIDAE
Paper Bubbles
Common Name: Swollen Bubble
Scientific Name:
Hydatina amplustre
(Linnaeus, 1758)
Adult Size: 22 mm
Depth: 2 - 10 feet
Notes: In sand

Family: HYDATINIDAE
Paper Bubbles
Common Name: Paper Bubble
Scientific Name: *Hydatina physis*
(Linnaeus, 1758)
Adult Size: 20 mm
Depth: 2 - 10 feet
Notes: In sand

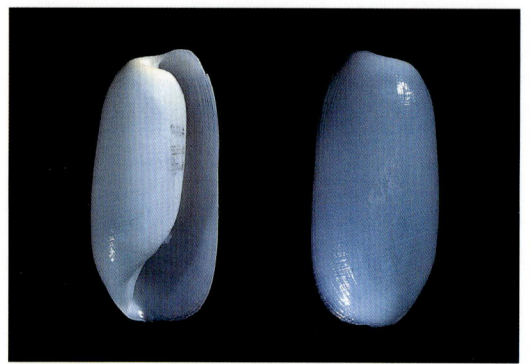

Family: CYLICHNIDAE
Cylindrical Bubbles
Common Name: Canoe Bubble
Scientific Name: *Cylichna pusilla*
(Pease, 1860)
Adult Size: 17 mm
Depth: 30 - 150 feet
Notes: In sand

Family: HAMINOEIDAE
White Bubbles
Common Name: Kuhn's Bubble
Scientific Name: *Atys kuhnsi*
Pilsbry, 1917
Adult Size: 21 mm
Depth: 50 - 120 feet
Notes: In sand

Family: BULLIDAE
True Bubbles
Common Name: Adam's Bubble
Scientific Name: *Bulla vernicosa*
Gould, 1859
Adult Size: 45 mm
Depth: 2 - 10 feet
Notes: In sand

CLASS GASTROPODA

CLASS BIVALVIA

45 *ARCIDAE* —
Ark Clams

CLASS BIVALVIA

45 ARCIDAE —
Ark Clams

This family is characterized by a shell the shape of folded bird wings and possessing many tiny teeth along the hinge plate. The hinge is flat or slightly concave and often as long as the shell. One of the most common species, *Arca ventricosa*, is most noticeable when its valves snap closed when it senses a disturbance. The shell then pulls itself abruptly down into a cavity it has hollowed out in the rock as it was growing, locking itself in place as a protection against predation. To feed, it raises itself up on its muscular foot and opens its valves enough to filter food from the water. Although very strongly attached to the rocks while nestled into their custom-built cavities, slipper lobsters are able to pry them loose. This often results in a large pile of empty ark shells outside the lobster's current shelter. Eagle rays have also been observed ripping them from the rocks.

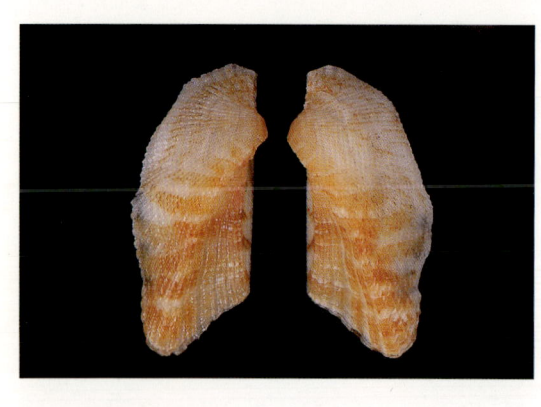

Common Name: Kauai Ark
Scientific Name: *Arca kauaia*
(Dall, Bartsch, and Rehder, 1938)
Adult Size: 18 mm
Depth: 150 - 300 feet
Notes: Dredged

Common Name: Ventricose Ark
Scientific Name: *Arca ventricosa*
Lamarck, 1819
Adult Size: 80 mm
Depth: 30 - 60 feet
Notes: On and in coral and rock

Common Name: Hawaiian Ark
Scientific Name:
Barbatia (Acar) divaricata
(Sowerby, 1833)
Adult Size: 38 mm
Depth: Intertidal to 600 feet
Notes: Under rocks and in cracks

CLASS BIVALVIA

GLYCYMERIDIDAE —
Bittersweet Clams

CLASS BIVALVIA

GLYCYMERIDIDAE —
Bittersweet Clams

The shells of the Glycymerididae are relatively thick, equivalved, and most have strong radiating chords with deep grooves which imparts a scalloped look to the edge of each valve. They live in sand and silt just beneath the surface and are easily picked up in dredges and trawl hauls. The Glycymerididae are deep-water bivalves in Hawaii and are rarely found on beaches here. In other areas of the tropical Indo-Pacific, they are common on beaches such as Kuta Beach on Bali in Indonesia, which has no barrier reef and a constant pounding surf.

Common Name: Walnut Clam
Scientific Name:
Glycymeris arcodentiens
(Dall, 1895)
Adult Size: 22 mm
Depth: 90 - 1000 feet
Notes: Trawled

Common Name: Albatross Clam
Scientific Name:
Glycymeris diomedea
Dall, Bartsch, and Rehder, 1938
Adult Size: 22 mm
Depth: 600 - 2000 feet
Notes: Trawled

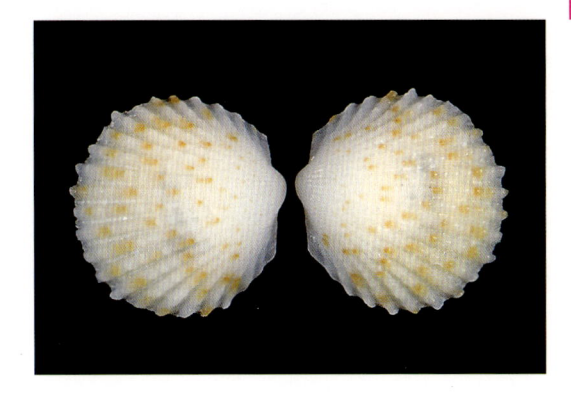

Common Name: Molokai Clam
Scientific Name:
Glycymeris molokaia
Dall, Bartsch, and Rehder, 1938
Adult Size: 7 mm
Depth: 180 - 1000 feet
Notes: Trawled

CLASS BIVALVIA

Common Name: Nut Clam
Scientific Name: *Glycymeris nux*
Dall, Bartsch, and Rehder, 1938
Adult Size: 20 mm
Depth: 60 - 1000 feet
Notes: Trawled

Common Name: Bittersweet Clam
Scientific Name: *Glycymeris* sp.
Adult Size: 22 mm
Depth: 1000 feet
Notes: Trawled

CLASS BIVALVIA

CLASS BIVALVIA

MYTILIDAE —
Marine Mussels

CLASS BIVALVIA

MYTILIDAE —
Marine Mussels

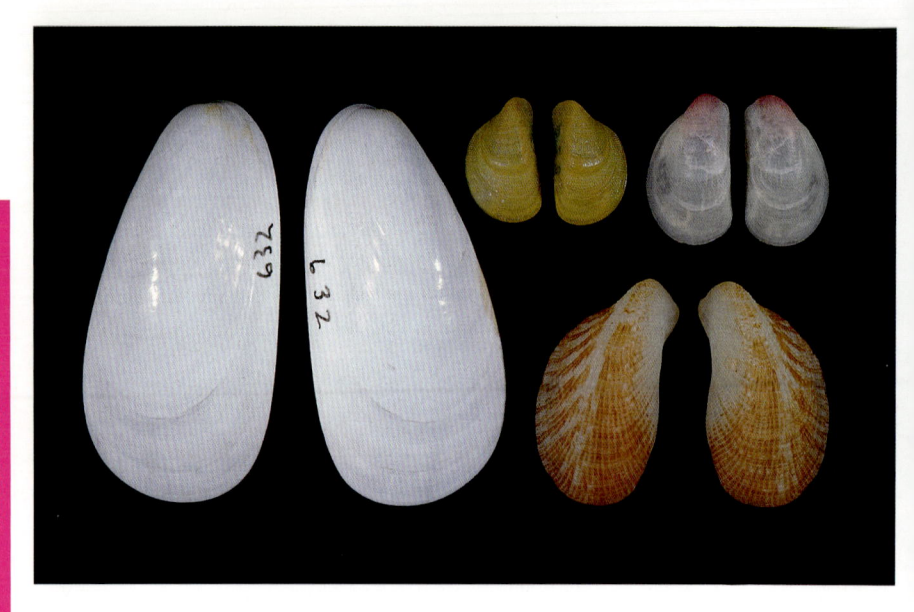

Members of the family Mytilidae live by one of four strategies. Some are sedentary, some bore deeply into coral formations, some are nest builders and some are commensal. They are all equivalved. The borers live deep inside the calcium skeleton of corals such as *Porites lobata,* and the tubes they bore are clearly visible in some large chunks of coral thrown up on beaches after storms. The commensal forms are small and thin-shelled due to their protected existence inside the bodies of ascidians. The sedentary species live by attaching themselves to a hard substrate such as a rock or pier piling, often congregating in densely-packed colonies. Each shell is anchored to the substrate by means of byssal threads that allow some flexibility of movement while holding the shells erect. They can also be found on drifting flotsam where the weight of the growing mussels may eventually sink their raft home. The nest builders use those same byssal threads to attach to pieces of coral and shells, together forming a protective nest. These are usually found on a soft substrates such as sandy silt or mud.

Common Name: Pease's Mussel
Scientific Name:
Amygdalum peasei
(Newcomb, 1870)
Adult Size: 38 mm
Depth: 2 - 30 feet
Notes: Live in colonies

Common Name: Bryan's Mussel
Scientific Name: *Septifer bryanae*
(Pilsbry, 1921)
Adult Size: 12 mm
Depth: Intertidal to 80 feet
Notes: Under rocks in tide pools and attached to reef flats

Common Name: Spatula Mussel
Scientific Name: *Septifer rudis*
Dall, Bartsch, and Rehder, 1938
Adult Size: 8 mm
Depth: 90 - 300 feet
Notes: Dredged

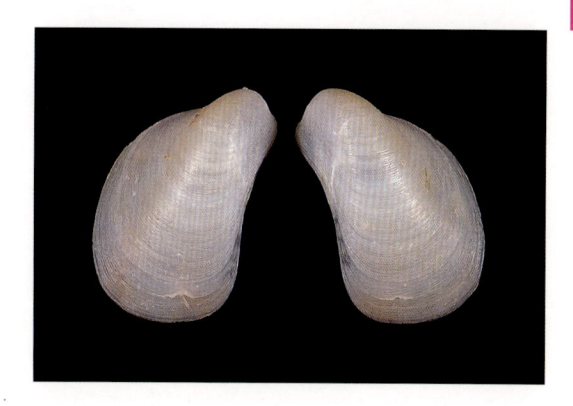

CLASS BIVALVIA

CLASS BIVALVIA

PINNIDAE —
Pen Shells

CLASS BIVALVIA

PINNIDAE —
Pen Shells

The Pinnidae live buried in the bottom or occasionally underneath rocks where they can sometimes be found flattened to the contours of the rock. They are all sedentary, anchored by a cluster of byssal threads in the sand or to a rock. Most members of the family live buried up to their lip in sand or silt with one species, *Pinna muricata,* forming large, dense colonies that cover several acres of the bottom. These populations are often so dense that the shells are only millimeters apart. These large colonies in turn become habitat for a myriad of animals that are ordinarily quite rare, including *Strombus helli* and several species of *Cymatium,* which appear to feed on the pen shells. Worthy of mention is that after a continuous week of heavy waves pounding the coast during the 1980 storm, the *Pinna* beds on Maui disappeared and have not recovered. The valves, which do not close as tightly as in other bivalves, made the pen shells susceptible to fouling by the great sand movement that occurred during the storm, smothering them.

225

Common Name: Prickly Pen Shell
Scientific Name: *Pinna muricata*
Linnaeus, 1758
Adult Size: 110 mm
Depth: Intertidal to 300 feet
Notes: Buried in open sand

Common Name: Purse Pen Shell
Scientific Name:
Streptopinna saccata
(Linnaeus, 1758)
Adult Size: 100 mm
Depth: 3 - 60 feet
Notes: Buried in sand near rocks

CLASS BIVALVIA

PTERIIDAE —
Pearl Oysters

CLASS BIVALVIA

PTERIIDAE —
Pearl Oysters

The pearl oysters are named for their pearly, opalescent shell interior. This smooth lining, which is the hardest part of the shell, is created by very fine layers of aragonite, a form of calcium, which may consist of as many as 5,000 layers of crystals. When the mantle, which lays down this hard layer, becomes irritated by a foreign body such as a grain of sand or a parasite, it responds by smoothing over the irritant and sometimes completely encasing it in the "pearly" secretion, thus producing a pearl. While pearls can be produced by many mollusks, the most desirable are produced by the pearl oysters. The production of the pearl is what gives the inner layer its most common name, "the mother-of-pearl." Some pearl oysters can be found attached to the reef while others can be seen attached to the limbs of black corals where they are suspended off the bottom. This provides a cleaner, steadier flow of water to filter for their food, and raises them out of reach of bottom-dwelling predators. Pearl Harbor was named for a pearl oyster, Pinctada radiata, which once lived there in numbers.

Common Name: Black-lipped Pearl Oyster
Scientific Name:
Pinctada margaritifera
(Linnaeus, 1758)
Adult Size: 290 mm
Depth: 2 - 60 feet
Notes: Attached to rocks and fossil corals. Often oriented vertically

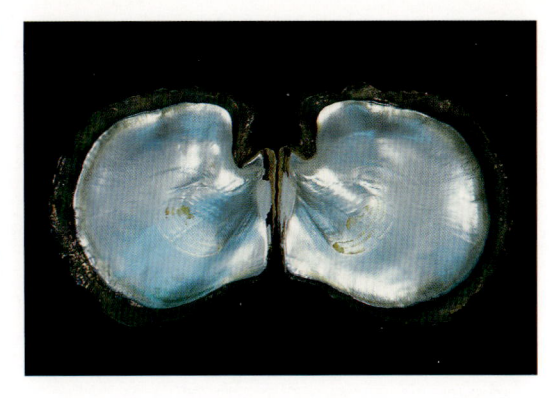

Common Name: Black Coral Oyster
Scientific Name: *Pteria brunnea*
(Pease, 1836)
Adult Size: 95 mm
Depth: 120 - 300 feet
Notes: Living on black corals

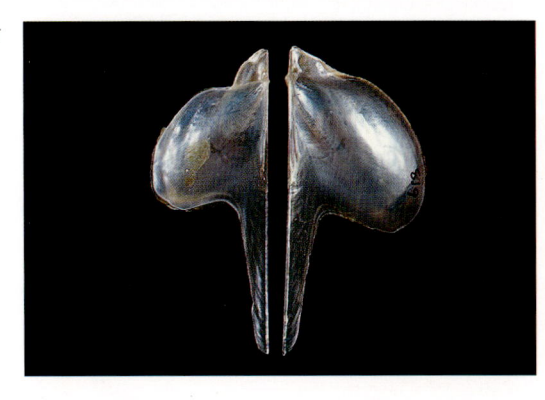

CLASS BIVALVIA

CLASS BIVALVIA

PECTINIDAE —
Scallops

CLASS BIVALVIA

CLASS BIVALVIA

PECTINIDAE — Scallops

Some scallops spend their lives attached to the bottom, often on the undersides of rocks where they filter water for their food, while other species simply lie out in the open on sand or mud bottoms. When a group of the latter is disturbed, they literally take flight, swimming away from the disturbance in a frantic scramble like a startled flock of birds. A single, huge adductor muscle allows the scallop to rapidly pump its valves together and jet away. This jet of water can be directed, allowing some control over the escape route. Just inside the scallop's two ruffled valves and arrayed along the very edge of the mantle that secretes the shell are hundreds of tiny blue eyes. These are the triggers that start the explosive swimming of the scallop and direct it to swim away from a detected disturbance. This same swimming mechanism produces a jet of water through the siphon, allowing it to dig out shallow depressions in the bottom in which to lie. Some species of scallops were used by Hawaiians to make head lei and hat bands.

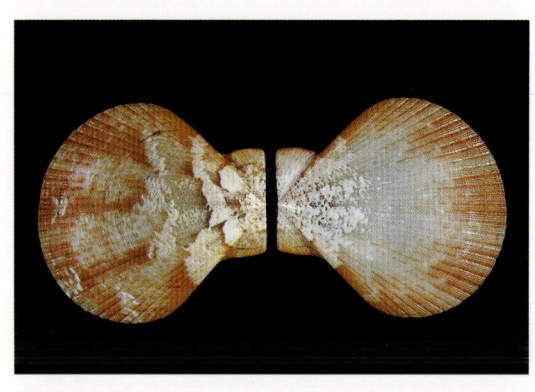

Common Name: Lambert's Pecten
Scientific Name:
Anguipecten lamberti
(Sowerby, 1874)
Adult Size: 29 mm
Depth: 90 - 2000 feet
Notes: Dredged

Common Name: Cooke's Pecten
Scientific Name:
Chlamys irregularis
(Sowerby, 1842)
Adult Size: 32 mm
Depth: 30 - 450 feet
Notes: Under rocks

Common Name: Langford's Pecten
Scientific Name:
Decatopecten noduliferum
(Sowerby, 1842)
Adult Size: 35 mm
Depth: 30 - 300 feet
Notes: On sand

Common Name: Judd's Pecten (E)
Scientific Name: *Haumea juddi*
Dall, Bartsch, and Rehder, 1938
Adult Size: 27 mm
Depth: 20 - 300 feet
Notes: On sand in colonies

Common Name: Waikiki Pecten
Scientific Name: *Pecten waikikius*
Dall, Bartsch, and Rehder, 1938
Adult Size: 40 mm
Depth: 3 - 600 feet
Notes: Dredged

CLASS BIVALVIA

CLASS BIVALVIA

SPONDYLIDAE —
Thorny Oysters

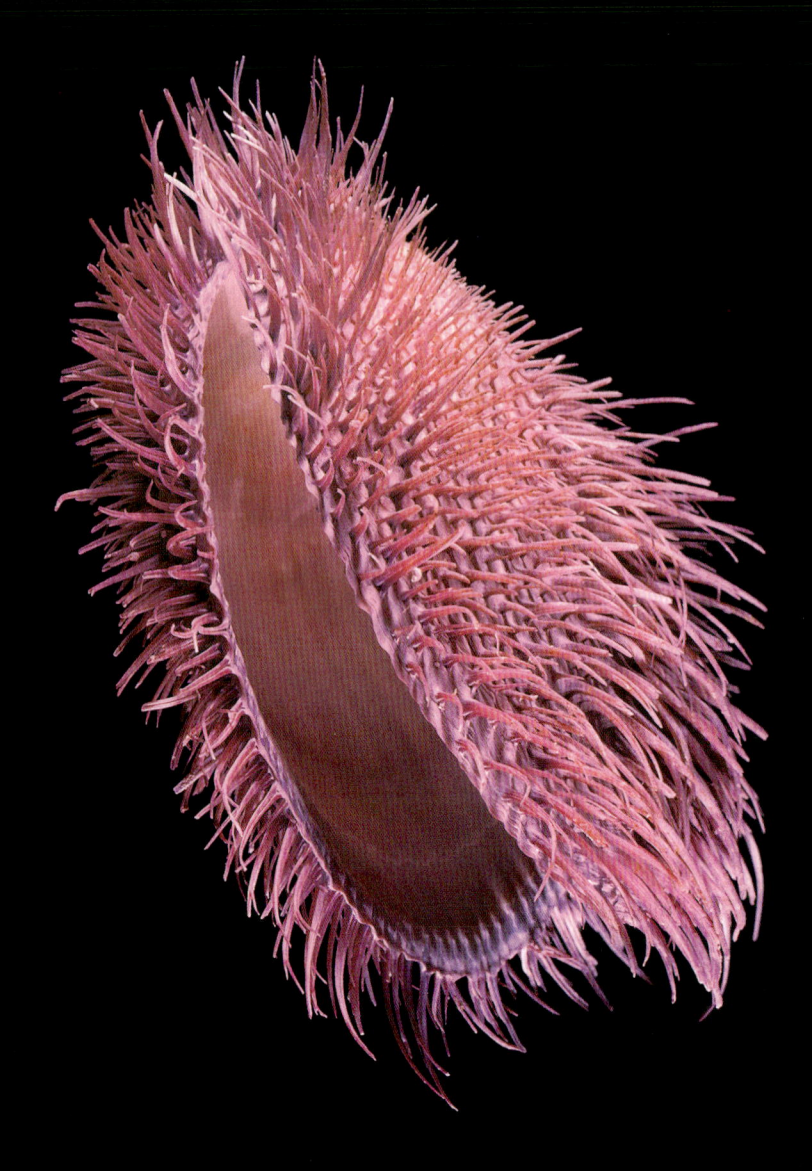

CLASS BIVALVIA

SPONDYLIDAE —
Thorny Oysters

The species in this group are difficult to identify because each shell is so variable. Each oyster, being cemented to one spot on the reef for life, encounters different environmental influences such as space limitations, nutrient content of the water and amount of water movement. Therefore, each shell can look quite different from another of the same species and will not necessarily be symmetrical as are most other groups of bivalves. The many fine or heavy spines protect the animal along the edge from attacks by fish. They also allow places of attachment for algae, tube worms, sponges, etc. which may aid in camouflage, but also add to the difficulty in identification. The shells of this group may be vividly colored or encrusted so much that they are indistinguishable from rock. Often, the only way to spot the large Hawaiian spiny oyster is to come upon a slipper lobster perched on top of it in the process of opening it to eat. The animal inside the shells may be plain or colorful as well. Ruffled, vivid animals with many silver, light-sensitive "eyes" along the open edge of the oyster are mesmerizing to watch.

Common Name: Cat's Tongue Oyster
Scientific Name:
Spondylus linguaefelis
Sowerby, 1847
Adult Size: 110 mm
Depth: 30 - 250 feet
Notes: In shaded areas such as under ledges, in cracks and along drop-offs

Common Name: Nicobar Thorny Oyster
Scientific Name:
Spondylus nicobaricus
Schreibers, 1793
Adult Size: 40 mm
Depth: 10 - 350 feet
Notes: In shaded areas such as under ledges, in cracks and along drop-offs

Common Name: Hawaiian Thorny Oyster
Scientific Name:
Spondylus violacescens
Lamarck, 1819
Adult Size: 100 mm
Depth: Intertidal to 100 feet
Notes: Attached to rocks in tide pools and beyond the reef on rocks and walls

CLASS BIVALVIA

52   *LIMIDAE* —
File Clams

CLASS BIVALVIA

52　LIMIDAE —
File Clams

Living file clams are most recognized by their thin, delicately-sculpted white shells and the long red or white tentacles which line the mantle edge. Highly sensitive, the extended tentacles can warn of danger and also capture food. When swimming, these tentacles expand, adding apparent size to the shell and creating a beautiful pattern to an onlooking diver. The tentacles are also very sticky and can be dropped by the clam like a lizard drops its tail. A predator attacking the clam is likely to get a mouth full of tentacles for its efforts. File clams typically live under sand, under rocks or down inside dark crevices, and some can swim if disturbed. Clapping the valves together produces a jet of water that allows the clam to escape if a predator shows interest. A bottom-dwelling predator such as a sea star has no way of pursuing the jetting clam and wouldn't know which direction the clam had taken due to the sea star's lack of eyes. File clams are known to build nests created by fibers secreted from their mantle.

Common Name: White-tentacled File Shell
Scientific Name: *Lima keokea*
Dall, Bartsch, and Rehder, 1938
Adult Size: 32 mm
Depth: 50 - 200 feet
Notes: Attaches to undersides of rocks

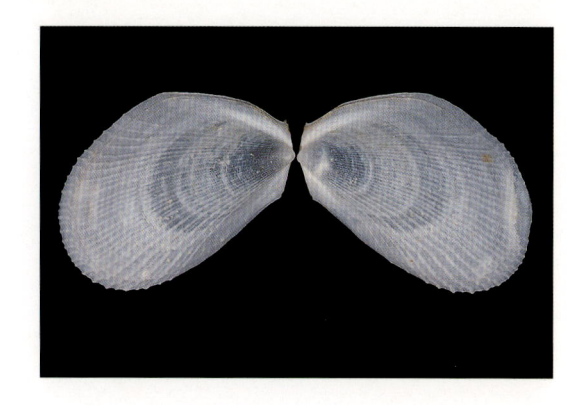

Common Name: Lahaina File Shell
Scientific Name: *Lima lahaina*
Dall, Bartsch, and Rehder, 1938
Adult Size: 35 mm
Depth: 50 - 300 feet
Notes: Found beneath rocks on sand

CLASS BIVALVIA

CLASS BIVALVIA

53 *CHAMIDAE* — Jewel Boxes

CLASS BIVALVIA

53   CHAMIDAE —
Jewel Boxes

The jewel boxes get their name from the upper valve of the shell which forms a lid inside the larger, lower valve. These shells are not mobile reef- or sediment-dwellers, but cement themselves to rocks or any other hard substrate. When growing on old metal shipwrecks they are sometimes shed along with the flaking rust of the hull and fall to the bottom. The shells from these old wrecks often have picked up minerals from the rusting metal and their shells can be orange, yellow, purple or even red. The variable colors combined with the concentric rows of spines make these shells very complex and interesting. They are all filter feeders and tend to live in colonies. Many factors may trigger spawning, including water temperature, tides and chemicals released by other clams. When spawning occurs, the water above these colonies appears to be filled with smoke as they all release their gametes into the water in synchrony increasing the chances of fertilization.

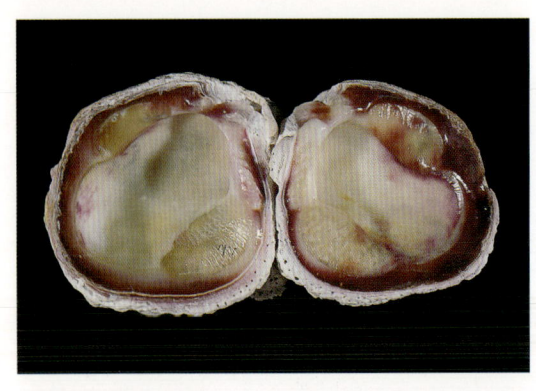

Common Name: Violet-mouth Jewel Box
Scientific Name: *Chama iostoma* Conrad, 1837
Adult Size: 40 mm
Depth: Intertidal to 300 feet
Notes: Attached to rocks in tide pools, on reef flats and beyond the reef

Common Name: Yellow Jewel Box
Scientific Name: *Chama* sp.
Adult Size: 50 mm
Depth: 120 feet
Notes: On wreck

CLASS BIVALVIA

LUCINIDAE —
Saucer Clams

CLASS BIVALVIA

CLASS BIVALVIA

LUCINIDAE —
Saucer Clams

The valves of the clams in the family Lucinidae are equivalved, strong, subcircular, white or yellow and lack a gloss, being somewhat chalky. The pattern of ridges and grooves on the valves is distinctive for each species. The shell, though broad, is not laterally thick, making it easier for the muscular foot to draw the clam through the substrate. Saucer Clams appear to not be too selective as to their habitat, with species being found in sand or mud. These shells are common in sand pockets in moderately shallow to deep water.

Common Name: Punctate Saucer Clam
Scientific Name: *Codakia punctata*
(Linnaeus, 1758)
Adult Size: 50 mm
Depth: 2 - 45 feet
Notes: In sand

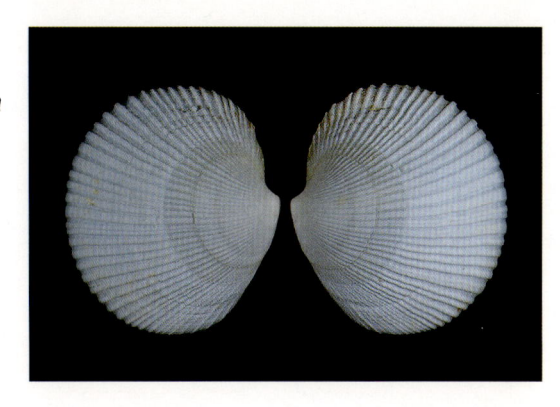

Common Name: Bella Saucer Clam
Scientific Name: *Ctena bella*
(Conrad, 1837)
Adult Size: 15 mm
Depth: Intertidal to 180 feet
Notes: In sand in tide pools, on reef flats and beyond the reef

Common Name: Transverse Saucer Clam
Scientific Name: *Ctena transversa*
Dall, Bartsch, and Rehder, 1938
Adult Size: 10 mm
Depth: 20 - 300 feet
Notes: Beneath rocks

CLASS BIVALVIA

CLASS BIVALVIA

55   *CARDIIDAE* —
Cockles

CLASS BIVALVIA

55 CARDIIDAE —
Cockles

Though some cockles have heavy, deeply-sculpted shells and others delicate, thin shells, all basically resemble a heart in shape, which led to their family name Cardiidae. Cockles are sand-dwellers which, like many other clams, laterally compress their foot so that it can be pushed deeply into the sand, then expand it to work as an anchor as the shell is pulled beneath the surface of the sand for protection. Once in a secure place, they extend their siphons back above the sand surface and draw a steady flow of water down to be filtered for food. Prominent interlocking teeth along the edges of the valves keep predators from getting inside, though sea stars simply grasp the shells from the outside and exert a continuous pull, tiring the muscle holding the shells together and eventually opening the clam far enough to insert its stomach and digest the living animal in its shell. While the sexes are separate in most bivalves, some cockle species possess both male and female reproductive organs.

Common Name: Hawaiian Cockle
Scientific Name:
Trachycardium orbita
(Sowerby, 1833)
Adult Size: 70 mm
Depth: 40 - 180 feet
Notes: Buried in sand pockets in shallow water

CLASS BIVALVIA

56 *TELLINIDAE* —
Tellin Clams

CLASS BIVALVIA

56 *TELLINIDAE* — Tellin Clams

Tellins are a shell collector's nightmare. There are many very beautiful and richly-colored species that make them one of the most colorful groups of bivalves, but there are also many small white species that are almost impossible to differentiate. Tellins are quite active, burrowing into the sand with their large foot and extending long siphons up to the surface, one to draw water down to be filtered for food and the other through which to exhale the water. In addition to filter feeding, some tellins will sometimes extend one very long siphon up onto the surface of the sand at low tide and "vacuum" deposit material which is sorted in the gills for anything edible. They will often move laterally beneath the sand while searching for new areas to feed after having exhausted the food in an area. The unusual shape and sculpture of the group may help to keep them from being pulled upward when the siphons are retracted.

Common Name: Sunset Tellin
Scientific Name: *Tellina crucigera*
Lamarck, 1818
Adult Size: 33 mm
Depth: 20 - 300 feet
Notes: Buried in sand

Common Name: Mussel-like Tellin
Scientific Name:
Tellina (Pharaonella) perna
(Spengler, 1798)
Adult Size: 62 mm
Depth: 45 - 90 feet
Notes: In fine sand

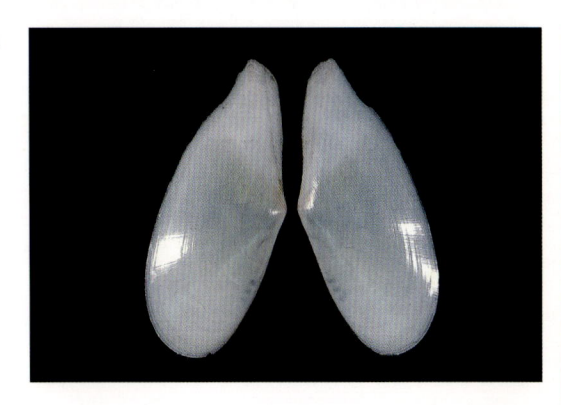

Common Name: Rasp Tellin
Scientific Name:
Tellina (Scutarcopagia) scobinata
Linnaeus, 1758
Adult Size: 60 mm
Depth: 30 - 50 feet
Notes: In sand pockets on reef flats

CLASS BIVALVIA

CLASS BIVALVIA

57 *PSAMMOBIIDAE* — Sunset Clams

CLASS BIVALVIA

57   PSAMMOBIIDAE —
Sunset Clams

If the family Psammobiidae had been described from Hawaii, it certainly would not have earned the common name, sunset clams. All of Hawaii's species are white or cream colored, rather than the rich colors found elsewhere in the world. Hawaii's Psammobiidids are found in deep water, where they live in silty or muddy substrate. The shells are elongate-ovate, compressed laterally and very thin and fragile. Some species have radiating sculpture present at the anterior end of the shell.

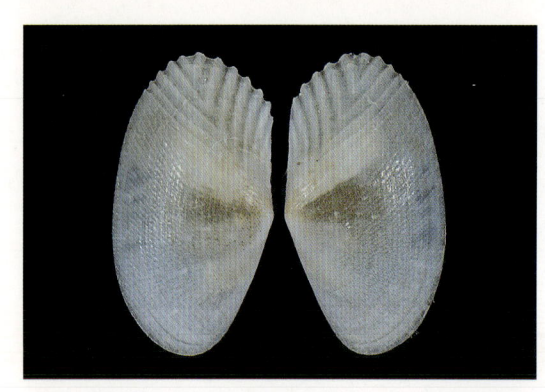

Common Name: Hawaiian Sunset Clam (E)
Scientific Name:
Grammatomya kanaka
(Pilsbry, 1921)
Adult Size: 17 mm
Depth: 3 - 300 feet
Notes: In sand

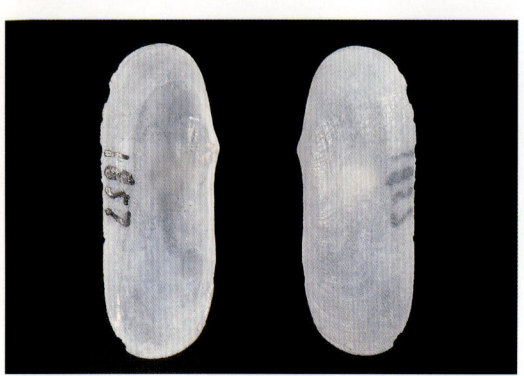

Common Name: Baldwin's Sunset Clam
Scientific Name:
Solecurtus baldwini
Dall, Bartsch, and Rehder, 1938
Adult Size: 19 mm
Depth: 300 - 1500 feet
Notes: Dredged

CLASS BIVALVIA

58   GLOSSIDAE —
Oxheart Clams

CLASS BIVALVIA

58   GLOSSIDAE —
Oxheart Clams

The Glossidae have angular, moderately thick and polished shells with concentric sculpturing. In Hawaii the group is represented by only one species from moderately deep water, which, like all Glossidae, lives in silt or sand. It was common as the byproduct of a shrimp trawler operating between Maui and Molokai in depths of over 1000 feet.

Common Name: Hawaiian Oxheart Clam   (E)
Scientific Name: *Meiocardia hawaiana*
Dall, Bartsch, and Rehder, 1938
Adult Size: 18 mm
Depth: 90 - 1000 feet
Notes: Trawled

CLASS BIVALVIA

59 *VENERIDAE* —
Venus Clams

CLASS BIVALVIA

59 *VENERIDAE* —
Venus Clams

The Venus clam family has been very successful and includes hundreds of species. These clams have thick, hard shells which are generally substantial enough to survive being washed up on beaches and are thus commonly found by beachcombers even in areas of high surf. They live a sedentary life well-anchored just beneath the surface of sand or mud. From this well-anchored position, they extend a siphon up to the surface of the sand through which water is draw for respiration, and from which to filter food. Most of the food consists of microscopic algae which live as plankton. The algae, as well as assorted other items, are trapped by mucus and must be sorted for digestion or disposal. The bold sculpture of some species indicates the clam most likely lives in sand and may be occasionally subjected to heavy surf where the sculpturing may help to keep them in position while they feed. The almost glassy smooth species are found in finer sand or mud bottoms in protected areas.

Common Name: Lettered Clam
Scientific Name:
Lioconcha hieroglyphica
(Conrad, 1837)
Adult Size: 42 mm
Depth: 3 - 300 feet
Notes: In sand

Common Name: Reticulated Venus Clam
Scientific Name:
Periglypta reticulata
(Linnaeus, 1758)
Adult Size: 65 mm
Depth: 5 - 60 feet
Notes: Buried deep in sand

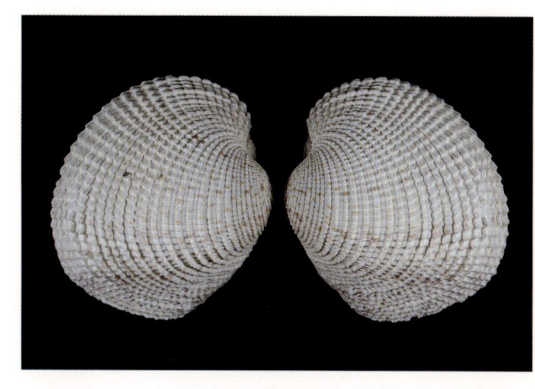

Common Name: Embossed Venus Clam
Scientific Name: *Venus toreuma* Gould, 1850
Adult Size: 37 mm
Depth: 30 - 1500 feet
Notes: In sand

CLASS BIVALVIA

# CLASS SCAPHOPODA

62 *DENTALIIDAE* —
Tusk Shells

CLASS SCAPHOPODA

62 DENTALIIDAE —
Tusk Shells

Tusk shells, which look like miniature elephant tusks, live buried more-or-less vertically in sand. Their shells are open at both ends. The tapered end projects just above the sand surface where water is circulated into a long mantle cavity for breathing and waste removal. After several minutes of very slow water inhalation, muscular contraction of the foot expels the water from the same opening. The foot protrudes from the opposite end. Once the tusk shell has burrowed into the sand, contractions and extensions of the foot pack the sand, creating a small cavity in which the tusk shell can feed. Long tentacles extend from the head and explore the cavity for organic debris, foraminiferans and bivalve larvae which stick to the adhesive ends of the tentacles and are passed back to the mouth. Living tusk shells are rarely seen because they remain under sand and live in deep water.

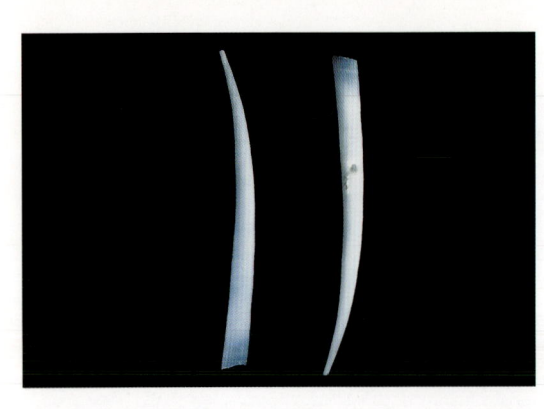

Common Name: Tusk Shell
Scientific Name: *Dentalium* sp.
Adult Size: 30 mm
Depth: 200 - 1000 feet
Notes: Trawled

CLASS SCAPHOPODA

Glossary

anterior - at or toward the head or front

ascidians - a class of marine animals of the Subphylum Urochordata (tunicates), which live attached to the bottom and are characterized by a thick mantle called the tunic. Sea squirts

byssal threads - adhesive threads secreted by some bivalves for use in attachment to the substrate

commensal - a species which obtains food, shelter or other benefits without affecting the other, or host, species

coralline algae - seaweeds which deposit calcium carbonate

detritus - dead organic matter and the decomposers of that matter

endemic - restricted to a particular region

intertidal - the zone between the lowest and highest tide

mantle - the outer layer of tissue in most mollusks that secretes the animal's shell

operculum - the protective horny plate which forms a barrier when a snail withdraws into its shell

papillae - nipple-like projections

phylogenetic - along the lines of descent or evolutionary development

posterior - at or toward the rear

precious corals - corals of the order Gorgonacea. Includes sea fans and sea whips

supratidal - above the high tide mark

umbilicus - a navel-like depression

urchin test - the exoskeleton of a sea urchin

valves - the two shells of bivalves

About the Author

Specializing in the Hawaiian mollusks, photographer/biologist Mike Severns has studied Hawaiian marine and land shells for over 30 years. His extensive Hawaiian marine shell collection includes many rare species from exceptionally deep water as well as tiny microshells so small that they are mounted on microscope slides in order to view. His land snail studies have required helicoptering into remote areas of the West Maui mountains and have resulted in the formulation of a mechanism which explains the current distribution of isolated populations of Hawaiian tree snails (paper in progress).

As a photographer and writer, Mike has published five books and contributed to many other books and articles, especially concerning Indonesian and Hawaiian marine animals. His underwater photography books include *Molokini Island, Hawaii's Premier Marine Preserve,* a full color book documenting Molokini's rich underwater environment and *Sulawesi Seas, Indonesia's Magnificent Underwater Realm,* an art book of his underwater photography designed by David Pickell.

Mike and his wife Pauline Fiene-Severns are owners of Mike Severns Diving, a charter boat operation on Maui celebrating their 21st year in business. Trips are designed around the animals and in-depth natural history briefings are conducted before the dives. They also have 12 years of experience leading natural history dive trips in Indonesia.

COMMON NAMES INDEX

Abbreviated Cone 176
Adam's Bubble 213
Agate Auger 192
Albatross Clam 219
Amanda's Auger 193
Apple Tun 79
Approximate Miter 164
Ark Clams 214, 215
Arrow Cone 182
Arrow Moon Shell 71
Articulate Horn 39
Augers 187, 188
Babylon Auger 194
Baldwin's Sunset Clam 254
Banded Cone 176
Banded Horn 39
Banded Spindle 135
Barrel Tun 79
Basket Miter 162
Basket Murex 110
Basket Shells 127, 128
Beaked Horn 39
Beck's Cowrie 56
Bella Dove Shell 140
Bella Saucer Clam 245
Bittersweet Clam 220
Bittersweet Clams 217, 218
Black Coral Oyster 229
Black Miter 156
Black-lipped Pearl Oyster 229
Black-mouthed Limpet 18
Black-mouthed Tun 79
Blood-spotted Frog Shell 90
Blue Dove Shell 139
Brown Scaly Drupe 115
Brown Spindle 136
Brown Turrid 171
Bryan's Obelisk 94
Bryan's Mussel 223
Bubble Cone 177
Bubble Helmet 76
Bullinids 207, 208

Burgess' -Distorsio 87
Burned Basket 129
Butterfly Moon Shell 71
Calf Cone 183
Calf Cowrie 63
Canoe Bubble 212
Carnelian Cowrie 61
Carrier Shells 45, 46
Cat Cone 177
Cat's Tongue Oyster 236
Chain Miter 165
Chaldean Cone 177
Checkered Cowrie 61
Cheerful Moon Shell 71
Chick-Pea Cowrie 64
Children's Cowrie 60
Chinese Cowrie 60
Chinese Horn 40
Circumactus Cone 178
Clear Sundial 202
Coat-of-Mail Shells 13, 14
Cockles 246, 247
Colored Wentletrap 103
Column Auger 195
Column Horn 38
Common Distorsio 87
Common Harp 149
Conchs 41, 42
Cone Shells 173, 174
Contracted Miter 154
Cooke's Pecten 232
Coral Shell 120, 122
Coral Shells 118, 119
Cornellian Pyramid 206
Cowries 52, 53
Crenulate Auger 195
Crenulate Miter 156
Crested Turrid 170
Cuming's Miter 165
Cuming's Turrid 171
Cylindrical Bubbles 210, 211
Dark-spotted Auger 193

265

Dawn Miter 154	Granulate Drupe 115
Distant Cone 178	Grape Drupe 116
Divided Auger 196	Green Chiton 15
Doncorn's Top Shell 24	Green-mouthed Spindle 135
Dove Shells 137, 138	Grooved Helmet 76
Dwarf Janthina 106	Grooved Tooth Cowrie 63
Edgar's Trivia 50	Hairy Triton 85
Eight-sided Limpet 21	Half-swimmer Cowrie 60
Eight-keeled Sundial 203	Halo Miter 166
Elegant Miter 165	Harmonious Triphorid 98
Elephant's Foot Moon Shell 72	**Harp Shells** 147, 148
Elongate Murex 110	Hatchet Pyramid 206
Elongate Triphorid 99	Hawaiian Ark 216
Embossed Venus Clam 259	Hawaiian Burnt Murex 109
Emerson's Miter 158	Hawaiian Cockle 248
Episcopal Miter 152	Hawaiian Hairy Triton 84
Eroded Coral Shell 120	Hawaiian Keyhole Limpet 21
Eroded Cowrie 57	Hawaiian Limpet 18
False Necklace Turrid 169	Hawaiian Nubila 153
False Tritons 141, 142	Hawaiian Olive 146
Fiery Miter 166	Hawaiian Oxheart Clam 256
Fiery Whelk 126	Hawaiian Spindle 133
File Clams 237, 238	Hawaiian Thorny Oyster 236
Flag Cone 186	Hawaiian Stromb 44
Flag Rock Shell 117	Hawaiian Sunset Clam 254
Flea Cone 183	Hawaiian Turban 28
Flesh-colored Miter 157	Hebrew Cone 179
Flour Whelk 125	Hectic Auger 189
Francolin Rock Shell 116	Hell's Stromb 43
Fringed Coral Shell 120	**Helmet Shells** 73, 74
Fringed Cowrie 65	Honey Cowrie 58
Frog Shells 88, 89	**Horn Shells** 36, 37
Funnel Auger 197	Horn-shaped Turrid 171
Furrow Pyramid 206	Horned Helmet 75
Gaskoin's Cowrie 56	Humpback Cowrie 64
Gaudy Basket 129	Imperial Cone 180
Gem Triton 84	Incised Triphorid 99
Girdled Triphorid 99	Inconstant Auger 190
Globose Janthina 106	Inflated Miter 155
Glossy Triphorid 98	Intermediate Dye Shell 117
Gold-banded Spindle 135	Isabelle's Cowrie 61
Goodwin's Harp 149	Japanese Coral Shell 122
Gould's Auger 189	Jester Cowrie 64
Granite Miter 158	**Jewel Boxes** 240, 241
Granulate Frog Shell 90	Judd's Pecten 233
Granulated Cowrie 58	Kauai Ark 216

Keyhole Limpets 19, 20	**Murex Shells** 107, 108
Kilburn's Auger 197	Mussel-like Tellin 251
King's Turrid 171	Necklace Turrid 169
Knobbed Turrid 172	**Nerites** 30, 31
Knobby Spindle 134	Newcomb's Miter 159
Knobby Triton 83	Nicobar Spindle 133
Kurose Spindle 134	Nicobar Thorny Oyster 236
Kuhn's Bubble 213	Nicobar Triton 884
Lahaina File Shell 239	Nodose Miter 164
Lambert's Pecten 232	Nuclear Cowrie 59
Lance Auger 190	Nussatella Cone 182
Langford's Miter 159	Nut Clam 220
Langford's Pecten 232	Oak Cone 184
Large-lipped Triton 86	Obelisk 94, 95
Lead Auger 191	**Obelisk Shells** 92, 93
Leopard Cone 180	Obscure Cone 182
Lesser Girdled Triton 86	Obscure Serpent 143
Lettered Clam 259	Ocellate Top Shell 24
Leviathan Cowrie 62	Oily Miter 156
Lined Bubble 209	**Olive Shells** 144, 145
Linsley's Chiton 15	Olive-shaped Miter 158
Literary Cone 179	Olomea Basket 130
Livid Cone 181	One-banded Miter 163
Love Harp 149	Opaque Moon Shell 72
Lynx Cowrie 62	Open Dye Shell 117
Many-colored Rock Shell 116	Ostergaard's Cowrie 59
Marbled Top Shell 25	Overhanging Horn 38
Margarite's Dove Shell 140	**Ovulids** 66, 67
Marie's Cowrie 55	**Oxheart Clams** 255, 256
Marine Mussels 221, 222	Pacific Miter 163
Marlinspike Auger 198	Pagoda Triphorid 100
Marriage Cone 296	Painted Wentletrap 103
Maui Miter 152	Papal Miter 153
Maui Spindle 133	Paper Bubble 212
Maui's Cowrie 65	**Paper Bubbles** 210, 211
Miser Dove Shell 139	Partridge Tun 80
Miters 150, 151	Pear-shaped Moon Shell 72
Moana Miter 163	**Pearl Oysters** 227, 228
Modest Miter 157	Pease's Periwinkle 35
Modest Pupa 209	Pease's Mussel 223
Mole Cowrie 65	Pele's Murex 109
Molokai Clam 219	**Pen Shells** 224, 225
Money Cowrie 58	Pencil Auger 191
Moon Shells 69, 70	Perforated Auger 199
Morelet's Cone 181	Perforated Cone 183
Mulberry Drupe 114	**Periwinkles** 33, 34

Peron's Carrier Shell 47	Saucer Clams 243, 244
Pheasant Shells 26, 27	Sazanka's Cone 185
Pimpled Basket 130	**Scallops** 230, 231
Pipipi Nerite 32	Scaly Spindle 136
Pleasant Auger 193	Schilders' Cowrie 62
Pleated Nerite 32	Schilders' Ovulid 68
Pointed Cone 176	Scripted Cone 180
Pointed Serpent 143	Shiny Auger 198
Polished Nerite 32	Short-whorled Auger 194
Polished Turrid 169	Similar Auger 192
Ponderous Helmet 75	Simple Miter 152
Pontifical Miter 153	Small Trivia 50
Porous Cowrie 59	Smooth Spindle 134
Praised Auger 190	Snake's Head Cowrie 57
Prickly Horn 38	Soldier Cone 181
Prickly Pen Shell 226	Spalding's Auger 194
Projecting Murex 109	Spatula Mussel 223
Punctate Saucer Clam 245	Speckled Periwinkle 35
Pupa Shells 207, 208	Spicer's Cone 178
Purple Janthina 106	**Spindle Shells** 131, 132
Purple Sea Snails 104, 105	Spotted Stromb 43
Purse Pen Shell 226	Spotted Vitularia 111
Purtymun's Miter 157	Sterk's Sundial 202
Pygmy Auger 199	Strawberry Drupe 114
Pyramld Shells 204, 205	Strawberry Miter 155
Radiating Sundial 203	Strawberry Whelk 125
Rashleigh's Cowrie 55	Striated Cone 185
Rasp Tellin 251	**Sundials** 200, 201
Rat Cone 184	**Sunset Clams** 252, 253
Red Triton 85	Sunset Tellin 251
Red-cloud Auger 198	Sutured Cone 186
Red-mouthed Frog Shell 91	Swollen Bubble 212
Reeve's Hairy Triton 83	Talc Limpet 18
Related Turrid 170	Tapering Cowrie 55
Reticulated Cowrie 63	**Tellin Clams** 249, 250
Reticulated Venus Clam 259	Tessellate Pupa 209
Retiform Cone 184	Textile Cone 186
Ribbed Miters 160, 161	Thaanum's Auger 189
Ribbed Whelk 125	Thaanum's Miter 162
Rival Triphorid 98	Thaanum's Obelisk 94
Robillard's Turrid 174	**Thorny Oysters** 234, 235
Rock Shells 112, 113	Three-toothed Stromb 43
Rough Basket 129	Three-winged Murex 110
Rough Periwinkle 35	Tiger Auger 196
Ruby-belted Turban 28	Tiger Cowrie 56
Rusty Miter 154	Tiny Distorsio 87

Tiny Triton	86
Top Shell	24, 25
Top Shells	22, 23
Transparent Trivia	50
Transverse Saucer Clam	245
Triphorids	96, 97
Triton's Trumpet	83
Tritons	81, 82
Trivias	48, 49
True Bubbles	210, 211
True Conchs	41, 42
True Limpets	16, 17
Tuberose Miter	166
Tun Shells	77, 78
Turban Shells	26, 27
Turrids	167, 168
Turtle-dove Dove Shell	139
Tusk Shell	262
Tusk Shells	260, 261
Twisted Serpent	143
Variable Dove Shell	140
Variable Pheasant Shell	29
Varicose Wentletrap	103
Variegated Sundial	202
Veil Drupe	114
Ventricose Ark	216
Venus Clams	257, 258
Verreaux's Auger	191
Vibex Helmet	75
Violet Coral Shell	121
Violet-mouth Whelk	126
Violet-mouth Jewel Box	242
Virgin Auger	199
Waikiki Pecten	233
Walnut Clam	219
War Miter	162
Wart Turban	28
Warty Frog Shell	90
Wasp Triton	85
Warty Miter	159
Waxy Cowrie	57
Weaver's Ovulid	68
Weaver's Turrid	170
Wentletraps	101, 102
Whelks	123, 124
White Auger	192
White Bubbles	210, 211
White-mouth Miter	155
White-ribbed Trivia	50
White-spotted Auger	197
White-tentacled File Shell	239
Wine-mouthed Frog Shell	91
Wolfe's Miter	164
Yellow Auger	195
Yellow Cone	179
Yellow Jewel Box	242
Yellow-banded Auger	196
Yellow-mouth Drupe	115

SCIENTIFIC NAMES INDEX

Classes are in bold type and end in "a." Families are in all capital letters and end in "dae." Subgenus and Genus are capitalized and italicized. Species and subspecies begin with a lower case letter and are italicized.

abbreviatus, Conus 176
Acar 216
achates, Terebra *192*
ACTAEONIDAE 207, 208
acutangulus, Conus 176
aemulans, Iniforis 98
affinis, Terebra *192*
alapapilionis, Natica 71
albula, Terebra *192*
Alcyna 24
amanda, Terebra 193
amiges, Cypraea chinensis 60
amoena, Terebra 193
amouretta, Harpa 149
amplustre, Hydatina 212
Amygdalum 223
Anachis 139
anatomica, Homolocantha 109
Anguipecten 232
Annepona 55
anus, Distorsio 87
aperta, Purpura 117
approximatum, Vexillum 164
aquatile, Cymatium 83
Arca 216
Architectonica 202
ARCHITECTONICIDAE 200, 201
ARCIDAE 214, 215
arcodentiens, Glycymeris 219
areolata, Terebra 193
argus, Terebra 194
articulata, Rhinoclavis 39
assimilis, Mitra 156
Aspella 109
Atys 213

aurora, Mitra 154
Babelomurex 120
babylonia, Terebra 194
Balcis 94, 95
baldwini, Solecurtus 254
bandanus, Conus 176
Barbatia 216
beckii, Cypraea 56
bella, Ctena 245
bella, Mitrella 140
bellum, Vexillum 162
bijubata, Turridrupa 170
Bittium 38
Bivalvia 214–259
Blasicrura 55
brachygyra, Terebra argus 194
brunnea, Pteria 229
bryani, Balcis 94
bryanae, Septifer 223
BUCCINIDAE 123, 124
bufonia, Bursa 90
Bulla 76, 213
bulla, Phalium 76
bullatus, Conus 177
BULLIDAE 210, 211
Bullina 209
BULLINIDAE 207, 208
burgessi, Distorsio 87
Bursa 90, 91
BURSIDAE 88, 89
Calliostoma 24
cancellarioides, Vexillum 164
Cancilla 157, 158
Cantharus 125
caputophidii, Cypraea caputserpentis 57
caputserpentis, Cypraea 57
CARDIIDAE 246, 247
carneola, Cypraea 61
carnicolor, Cancilla 157
Casmaria 75
CASSIDAE 73, 74
Cassis 75

270

castanella, Xenoturris 171
catenatum, Vexillum 165
catus, Conus 177
Cellana 18
cerithiformis, Xenoturris 171
CERITHIIDAE 36, 37
cerithina, Terebra 194
Cerithium 38, 39
cernica, Cypraea 57
chaldeus, Conus 177
Chama 242
CHAMIDAE 240, 241
Charonia 83
Chicoreus 109
childreni, Cypraea 60
chinensis, Cypraea 60
CHITONIDAE 13, 14, 15
Chlamys 232
chlorata, Terebra 195
chlorostoma, Peristernia 135
cicercula, Cypraea 64
cingulifera, Mastonia 99
circumactus, Conus 178
Cirsotrema 103
clathrus, Neocancilla 158
CLAVINIDAE 167, 168
Clavus 172
Clivipollia 125
Codakia 245
coelinae, Conus 178
Colubraria 143
COLUBRARIIDAE 141, 142
COLUMBELLIDAE 137, 138
columellaris, Terebra 195
columna, Cerithium 38
concors, Iniforis 98
CONIDAE 173, 174
consobrina, Turridrupa 170
contracta, Mitra 154
controversa, Cypraea isabella 61
Conus 146–186
Coralliobia 120
Coralliophila 120, 121
CORALLIOPHILIDAE 118, 119
corbiculum, Vexillum 162
cornelliana, Turbonilla 206
cornuta, Cassis 75
costata, Clivipollia 125
Costellaria . . . . 162 - 164
COSTELLARIIDAE 160, 161
crematus, Nassarius 129
crenulata, Pterygia 156
crenulata, Terebra 195
Cribrarula 56
crucigera, Tellina 251
cruentata, Bursa 90
Ctena 245
cumingii, Tritonoturris 172
cumingii, Vexillum 165
Cylichna 212
CYLICHNIDAE 210, 211
Cymatium 83–86
Cypraea 55–65
CYPRAEIDAE 52, 53
Decatopecten 232
DENTALIIDAE 260, 261
Dentalium 262
dentatus, Strombus 43
dilecta, Emarginula 21
dimidiata, Terebra 196
Diodora 21
diomedea, Glycymeris 219
distans, Conus 178
Distorsio 87
divaricata, Barbatia 216
dolabrata, Pyramidella 206
dolium, Tonna 79
Domiporta 157, 158
doncorni, Calliostoma 24
Drupa 114
Drupella 115
ebraeus, Conus 179
echinatum, Cerithium 38
edgari, Trivia 50
elata, Drupella 115
elongata, Viriola 99
elongatus, Pterynotus 110
Emarginula 21
EPITONIIDAE 101, 102
Epitonium 103
erinaceus, Casmaria 75
erosa, Coralliophila 120

271

erosa, Cypraea 57
Erosaria 56, 57, 58, 59, 60
Erronea 60
eugrammatus, Conus 179
EULIMIDAE 92, 93
Euplica 139, 140
exigua, Janthina 106
exigua, Trivia 50
farinosus, Cantharus 125
fasciata, Rhinoclavis 39
fasciatus, Latirulus 135
FASCIOLARIIDAE 131, 132
fastigium, Mitra 156
felina, Terebra 196
ferruginea, Mitra 154
fimbriata, Coralliobia 120
fimbriata, Cypraea 65
FISSURELLIDAE 19, 20, 21
flavidus, Conus 179
flavofasciata, Terebra 196
foliacea, Morula 115
fraga, Mitra 155
fragaria, Clivipollia 125
fucatum, Epitonium 103
fulvescens, Mitra 155
funiculata, Terebra 197
funiculus, Muricodrupa 110
Fusinus 133, 134
Fusolatirus 134
gaskoini, Cypraea 56
Gastropoda 16–213
gaudiosus, Nassarius 129
Gaza 24
Gelagna 86
Gemmula 169
Gibbula 25
globosa, Janthina 106
GLOSSIDAE 255, 256
GLYCYMERIDIDAE 217, 218
Glycymeris 219, 220
goodwini, Harpa 149
gouldi, Duplicaria 189
Grammatomya 254
granatina, Cancilla 158
granularis, Bursa 90
granulata, Cypraea 58

granulata, Morula 115
gualteriana, Natica 71
guttata, Terebra 197
Gutturnium 83
Gyrineum 86
HAMINOEIDAE 210, 211
Harpa 149
HARPIDAE 147, 148
Hastula 189, 190, 191
Haumea 233
hawaiana, Meiocardia 256
hawaiensis, Strombus vomer 44
hawaiiensis, Cypraea helvola . 58, 153
hawaiiensis, Mitra nubila 153
hectica, Hastula 189
Heliacus 202
helli, Strombus 43
helvola, Cypraea 58
hieroglyphica, Lioconcha 259
hilaris, Natica 71
Hiloa 29
hinuhinu, Iniforis 98
Hirtomurex 122
hirtus, Nassarius 129
Homolocantha 109
hordacea, Trivia 50
Hydatina 212
HYDATINIDAE 210, 211
ignea, Prodotia 126
Imbricaria 158
impendens, Bittium 38
imperialis, Conus 180
incisa, Viriola 99
incompta, Mitra 152
inconstans, Hastula 2-0
indica, Cypraea scurra 64
Iniforis 98
insularum, Chicoreus 109
intermedia, Thais 117
intermedium, Cymatium 884
interpolata, Gemmula 169
interstriatum, Vexillum 162
intextus, Trochus 25
iostoma, Chama 242
iostomus, Prodotia 126
Ipsa 60

irregularis, Chlamys 232	*maculatus, Strombus* 43
isabella, Cypraea 61	*maculifera, Cypraea* 63
ISCHNOCHITONIDAE 15	*major, Harpa* 149
Janthina 106	*Malea* 79
janthina, Janthina 106	*margarita, Mitrella* 140
JANTHINIDAE 104, 105	*margaritifera, Pinctada* 229
japonicus, Latiaxis 122	*Margovula* 68
juddi, Haumea 233	*mariae, Cypraea* 55
kalosmodix, Casmaria erinaceus .. 75	*marmorea, Gibbula* 25
kanaka, Grammatomya 254	*Mastonia* 99
kauaia, Arca 216	*matheroniana, Hastula* 190
keokea, Lima 239	*maui, Mitra* 152
kilburni, Terebra 197	*mauiensis, Cypraea* 65
kingae, Xenoturris 174	*Mauritia* 63, 64
kuhnsi, Atys 213	*mauritiana, Cypraea* 64
kuroseanus, Fusolatirus 134	*Meiocardia* 256
labiosum, Cymatium 86	*melanostoma, Cellana* 18
lahaina, Lima 239	*melanostoma, Tonna* 79
lamberti, Anguipecten 232	*melanostomus, Polinices* 72
lanceata, Hastula 190	*miles, Conus* 181
langfordiana 159	*miliaris, Vitularia* 111
Latiaxis 122	*miser, Anachis* 139
Latirulus 135	*Mitra* 152, 153, 154, 155, 156
Latirus 134, 135	*mitra, Mitra* 152
lautum, Vexillum 165	*Mitrella* 140
leopardus, Conus 180	MITRIDAE 150, 151
Leptothyra 28	*moelleri, Vexillum* 166
leucozonias, Vexillum 163	*molokaia, Glycymeris* 219
leviathan, Cypraea 62	*moneta, Cypraea* 58
Lima 239	*monilifera, Gemmula* 169
LIMIDAE 237, 238	*Monoplex* 83, 84, 85
Linatella 86	*moreleti, Conus* 181
lineata, Bullina 209	*Morula* 115, 116
linguaefelis, Spondylus 236	*morum, Drupa* 114
linsleyi, Rhyssoplax 15	*mundum, Cymatium* 84
Lioconcha 259	*muricata, Colubraria* 143
litoglyphus, Conus 180	*muricata, Pinna* 226
Littoraria 35	MURICIDAE 107, 108
LITTORINIDAE 33, 34	*muricinum, Cymatium* 83
livescens, Euplica 139	*Muricodrupa* 110
lividus, Conus 181	MYTILIDAE 221, 222
LUCINIDAE 243, 244	*Nassa* 116
Luria 61	NASSARIIDAE 127, 128
Lyncina 61, 62, 63	*Nassarius* 129, 130
lynx, Cypraea 62	*Natica* 71
maculata, Terebra 198	NATICIDAE 69, 70

273

Nebularia 154, 155	Periglypta 259
nebulosa, Terebra 198	Peristernia 135, 136
Neocancilla 158, 159	perna, Tellina 251
Nerita 32	peroniana, Xenophora 47
NERITIDAE 30, 31	PERSONIDAE 81, 82
newcombii, Scabricola 159	perspectiva, Architectonica 202
nicobaricum, Cymatium 84	pertusa, Terebra 199
nicobaricus, Fusinus 133	pertusus, Conus 186
nicobaricus, Spondylus 236	peselephanti, Polinices 72
nitida, Terebra 198	petaloides, Ischnochiton 15
nodatus, Latirus 134	Phalium 76
nodifera, Clavus 172	Pharaonella 251
noduliferum, Decatopecten 232	PHASIANELLIDAE 29
noumeensis, Latirus 135	Phenacovolva 68
nubila, Mitra 153	Philippia 203
nucleus, Cypraea 59	physis, Hydatina 212
nussatella, Conus 182	picea, Nerita 32
nux, Glycymeris 220	pileare, Cymatium 85
obscura, Colubraria 143	Pinaxia 116
obscurus, Conus 182	Pinctada 229
ocellata, Alcyna 24	Pinna 226
octagona, Diodora 21	PINNIDAE 224, 225
Oliva 146	pintado, Littoraria 35
olivaeformis, Imbricaria 158	planorbis, Conus 183
OLIVIDAE 144, 145	plicata, Nerita 32
olomea, Nassarius 130	plumbea, Hastula 191
orbita, Trachycardium 248	Polinices 72
ostergaardi, Cypraea 59	polita, Nerita 32
OVULIDAE 66, 67	**Polyplacophora** 13–15
oxytropis, Philippia 203	pomum, Malea 79
pacificum, Vexillum 163	ponderosa, Casmaria 75
pagoda, Viriola 100	poraria, Cypraea 59
papalis, Mitra 153	Prodotia 126
papilio, Neocancilla 159	producta, Aspella 109
papillosus, Nassarius 130	propinqua, Cypraea carneola 61
PATELLIDAE 16, 17, 18	PSAMMOBIIDAE 252, 253
paxillus, Oliva 146	pseudomonilifera, Gemmula 169
peasei, Amygdalum 223	Pteria 229
Peasiella 35	PTERIIDAE 227, 228
Pecten 233	Pterygia 156, 157
PECTINIDAE 230, 231	Pterynotus 110
pellucens, Cypraea teres 55	pudica, Pterygia 157
pellucidula, Trivia 51	pudica, Pupa 209
penicillata, Hastula 191	pulicarius, Conus 183
pennaceus, Conus 182	punctata, Codakia 245
perdix, Tonna 80	Pupa 209

Purpura 117
Purpuradusta 65
purtymuni, Pterygia 157
Pusia 164, 165, 166
pusilla, Cylichna 212
pusilla, Distorsio 87
pusillum, Gyrineum 86
Pustularia 64, 65
pygmaea, Terenolla 199
Pyramidella 206
PYRAMIDELLIDAE 204, 205
quercinus, Conus 184
radiata, Philippia 203
RANELLIDAE 81, 82
rashleighana, Cypraea 55
rattus, Conus 184
replicatum, Epitonium 103
reticulata, Periglypta 259
retifer, Conus 184
Rhinoclavis 39, 40
rhodostoma, Bursa 91
Rhyssoplax 15
ricina, Drupa 114
Ricinella 114
robillardi, Tritonoturris 172
rosa, Bursa 91
rostratum, Cerithium 39
rubeculum, Cymatium 85
rubricincta, Leptothyra 28
rubusidaeus, Drupa 114
rudis, Septifer 223
saccata, Streptopinna 226
sandvicensis, Fusinus 133
sandwicensis 18, 28, 146
sandwicensis, Cellana 18
sandwicensis, Oliva paxillus 146
sandwicensis, Turbo 28
sandwichensis, Conus suturatus . 186
sazanka, Conus 185
scabra, Littoraria 35
Scabricola 159
Scaphopoda 260–262
schilderorum, Cypraea 62
schilderorum, Margovula 68
scobinata, Tellina 251
scurra, Cypraea 64
Scutarcopagia 251
Semicassis 76
semiplota, Cypraea 60
Septa 85
Septifer 223
serta, Nassa 116
sinensis, Rhinoclavis 40
Solecurtus 254
Spendrillia 172
spiceri, Conus coelinae 178
SPONDYLIDAE 234, 235
Spondylus 236
sponsalis, Conus 185
squamosa, Peristernia 136
sterkii, Heliacus 202
stictica, Mitra 153
Streptopinna 226
striatus, Conus 185
Strigatella 156
strigilata, Hastula 191
STROMBIDAE 41, 42
Strombus 43, 44
Subcancilla 159
succincta, Linatella 86
sulcata, Pyramidella 206
sulcidentata, Cypraea 63
suturatus, Conus 186
Swainsonia 159
talcosa, Cellana 18
talpa, Cypraea 65
Talparia 65
tantilla, Peasiella 35
Tellina 251
TELLINIDAE 249, 250
Terebra 192, 193, 194, 195, 196,
                          197, 198, 199
TEREBRIDAE 187, 188
Terenolla 199
teres, Cypraea 55
tessellata, Cypraea 61
tessellata, Pupa 209
textile, Conus 186
thaanumi, Balcis 94
thaanumi, Duplicaria 189
THAIDIDAE 112, 113
Thais 117

tigris, Cypraea 56
Tonna 79, 80
TONNIDAE 77, 78
toreuma, Venus 259
tortuosa, Colubraria 143
Trachycardium 248
transversa, Ctena 245
Tricolia 29
TRIPHORIDAE 96, 97
tripterus, Pterynotus 110
Tristichotrochus 24
tritonis, Charonia 83
Tritonoturris 172
Trivia 50, 51
TRIVIIDAE 48, 49
TROCHIDAE 22, 23
Trochus 25
tuberosum, Vexillum 166
tumidus, Polinices 72
TURBINIDAE 26, 27, 28
Turbo 28
Turbonilla 206
turgida, Mitra 155
TURRIDAE 167, 168
Turridrupa 170
Turritriton 86
turturina, Euplica 139
umbilicatum, Phalium 76
unifascialis, Vexillum 166
unifasciatum, Vexillum 163
ustulata, Peristernia 136

uva, Morula 116
variabilis, Tricolia 29
varians, Euplica 140
varicosa, Cirsotrema 103
variegatus, Heliacus 202
VENERIDAE 257, 258
ventricosa, Arca 216
Venus 259
vernicosa, Bulla 213
verruca, Leptothyra 28
verrucosa, Subcancilla 159
versicolor, Pinaxia 116
vespaceum, Cymatium 85
Vexilla 117
Vexillum .117, 162, 163, 164, 165, 166
vexillum, Conus 186
vexillum, Vexilla 117
violacea, Coralliophila 121
violacescens, Spondylus 236
virgo, Terebra 199
Viriola 99, 100
vitellus, Cypraea 63
Vitularia 111
vomer, Strombus 44
waikikius, Pecten 233
weaveri, Phenacovolva 68
weaveri, Turridrupa 170
wolfei, Vexillum 164
Xenophora 47
XENOPHORIDAE 45, 46
Xenoturris 171

References and Further Reading

Abbott, R. Tucker & P. Dance. 1986. Compendium of Seashells. Melbourne, Florida: American Malacologists, Inc.

Bratcher, Twila & Walter O. Cernohorsky. 1987. Living Terebras of the World. Melbourne, Florida: American Malacologists, Inc.

Kay, E. Alison. 1979. Hawaiian Marine Shells. Honolulu: Bishop Museum Press.

Lalli, Carol M. & R. W. Gilmer. 1989. Pelagic Snails. Stanford: Stanford University Press.

Lorenz, Felix & A. Hubert. 1993. A Guide to Worldwide Cowries. Weisbaden, Germany: Verlag Christa Hemmen.

Moretzsohn, Fabio & E. Alison Kay, 1995. Hawaiian Marine Mollusks, an Update to Kay, 1979. Unpublished.

Paulay, Gustav. 1996. New Records and Synonymies of Hawaiian Bivalves (Mollusca). Records of the Hawaii Biological Survey for 1995. Bishop Museum Occasional Papers 45: 18-29.

Quirk, Stephen J. G. & C. Wolfe. 1974. Seashells of Hawaii. Honolulu: WW Distributors.

Rockel, Dieter, W. Korn & A. J. Kohn. 1995. Manual of the Living Conidae, vol. 1: Indo-Pacific Region. Weisbaden, Germany: Verlag Christa Hemmen.

Ruppert, Edward E. & Robert D. Barnes. 1994. Invertebrate Zoology. 6th Edition. Philadelphia: Saunders College Publishing.

Salisbury, Richard. 1998. Description of a new Hawaiian Pterygia: Pterygia purtymuni n.sp. (Gastropoda: Mitridae). La Conchiglia No. 289, October-December 1998; pp. 45-48.

Vermeij, Geerat J. 1993. A Natural History of Shells. Princeton: Princeton University Press.

Zeigler, Rowland F. & H. Porreca. 1969. Olive Shells of the World. W. Henrietta, New York: Zeigler and Porreca.